Compiled by Rashida Coleman-Hale

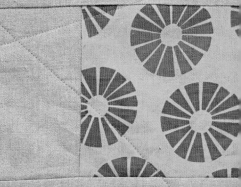

Zakka Style

24 Projects Stitched with Ease to Give, Use & Enjoy

stashBOOKS.
an imprint of C&T Publishing

Publisher: Amy Marson

Creative Director: Gailen Runge

Acquisitions Editor: Susanne Woods

Editor: Cynthia Bix

Technical Editors: Nanette S. Zeller,
Gailen Runge, and Carolyn Aune

Cover/Book Designer: Kristy Zacharias

Production Coordinator: Jenny Leicester

Production Editors: S. Michele Fry
and Alice Mace Nakanishi

Illustrators: Rashida Coleman-Hale
and Jenny Leicester

Photography by Christina Carty-Francis
and Diane Pedersen of C&T Publishing, Inc.,
unless otherwise noted

Published by Stash Books, an imprint of C&T Publishing, Inc., P.O. Box 1456, Lafayette, CA 94549

Library of Congress Cataloging-in-Publication Data

Coleman-Hale, Rashida.

Zakka style : 24 projects stitched with ease to give, use & enjoy / Rashida Coleman-Hale.

p. cm.

ISBN 978-1-60705-416-0 (soft cover)

1. Sewing. 2. Textile crafts. I. Title.

TT715.C645 2011

646--dc23

2011016996

Printed in China

10 9 8 7 6 5 4 3 2

Contents

ACKNOWLEDGMENTS

A huge, huge thank-you to *all* the designers who contributed to this project. Without your talent, style, and amazing skill, none of this would have been possible. You ladies rock!

Thank you to Susanne Woods for making this little dream a reality, to Cynthia Bix and Nanette S. Zeller for making sense of my organized confusion, and to everyone on the Stash Books team for their hard work and dedication.

Thank you to my dear hubby, Melvin, and our wee ones for being so supportive of me through all of this. You all are my everything.

And last but certainly not least, mega thanks to my dear grandfather. You raised me, you taught me what I know, you inspired me to do better. I only wish you were here to share this with me. This is for you. I love you, Grandpa.

RASHIDA COLEMAN-HALE has been making things ever since she can remember. Sewing is a gift passed on to her by her mother, grandmother, and grandfather, who was a tailor. Rashida studied fashion design at the Fashion Institute of Technology. Not sure if fashion was her calling, she traded her sewing machine for a computer and worked as a freelance graphic designer. Her passion for sewing was rekindled in 2006 after the arrival of her first child, and she began the blog "I Heart Linen" to document her reborn creative life and her life as a stay-at-home mommy.

Rashida spent much of her youth in Tokyo, Japan, where her love of linen began. Her experiences there have completely influenced her work and its style. Her work has been featured in *Sew News, Stitch, Sew Hip!, ReadyMade, Burda Style,* and *Quilting Arts* magazines, as well as on popular blogs such as Ohdeedoh.com, DesignSponge.com, Decor8.com, Craftzine.com, SewMamaSew.com, and TrueUp.com. Her first book, *I Love Patchwork,* was published in 2009.

Rashida lives in Atlanta with her husband and their three children. She is now a fabric designer for Timeless Treasures; her first collection debuted in the Spring of 2011. Read more about her crafty life at iheartlinen.typepad.com.

Introduction

During the many years I lived in Japan, I was fascinated by the popular zakka design movement, which had been in progress there for a long time. After school, I used to cruise through all the little zakka shops and just soak in everything. The Japanese zakka aesthetic has been a part of me ever since, and my love for that style has reemerged now that I am a crafter.

The term *zakka* has been loosely translated to mean "miscellaneous goods," "many things," or "sundries." But it has grown to mean a style that embodies a kind of simple charm and uniqueness—something handmade that is useful yet pleasing. Zakka has evolved into a design style that has become popular all over the world.

In my world, zakka style is not only an aesthetic but also almost a way of life. Making handcrafted gifts for friends and having handmade items in my home to share with my family make being able to sew such a wonderful thing.

This style also has been an inspiration to many other artists in recent years, especially in the blogging community. When I was brainstorming ideas for this book, it occurred to me—what better way to explore this phenomenon than to showcase the work of 24

of my favorite zakka artists from around the world! Each artist I have invited to contribute has created a project that brilliantly embodies her own zakka style in clever, innovative, whimsical, and fabulous ways. The projects featured range from things for your home to items you could easily make as last-minute gifts for a friend or loved one.

Handmade zakka sewing uses simple techniques, but the projects are innovative, useful, and lovely to look at. I hope this book will inspire you to explore your own zakka style and to learn some new sewing tricks along the way!

Rashida

Special Note

Many of the projects in this book feature linen. If you have trouble finding linen, you can use a decorator-weight textured solid or a linen/cotton blend. A lightweight canvas could also work.

Zigzag Tote

FINISHED: 14″ wide × 12″ high × 3″ deep

This linen tote bag is just laden with wonderful zigzaggy good-ness—a timeless design that will be loved for years to come. It's also the perfect size for taking along with you around town or when you're shopping for more fabric!

ARTIST: Lisa Billings

WEBSITE:

pinklemonadeboutique.etsy.com

Lisa lives right outside
Providence, Rhode Island,
with her husband, Jeff; her
daughter, Olivia; and her wacky
cat, Violet. She started quilting
about fifteen years ago and
is thrilled with how the craft
has really taken off in such a
modern and exciting direction.
Besides quilting, she loves to
experience the Providence
cultural scene and to cook (and
eat!), and she tries to keep up
with her Etsy shop, where she
sells her handbags.

Materials and Supplies

Yardages are based on 40˝-wide fabric.

Linen or textured solid fabric:
1 yard

Lining fabric: ¾ yard

Yellow accent fabric: ⅛ yard

Brown accent fabric: ⅛ yard

Fusible batting (such as Fusible
Fleece or Fusible Thermolam Plus
by Pellon): ½ yard

Firm fusible interfacing (such as
Décor-Bond Fusible Interfacing
by Pellon): ¾ yard

1 magnetic snap closure

Cutting

Linen:
Cut 1 strip 4¼˝ × width of
fabric; subcut into 6 squares
4¼˝ × 4¼˝, and then cut each
square twice diagonally to make
24 quarter-square triangles.

Cut 1 rectangle
13½˝ × 16½˝, for back.

Cut 1 rectangle 5˝ × 16½˝,
for left front panel.

Cut 1 rectangle 3½˝ × 16½˝,
for right front panel.

Cut 2 strips 2˝ × 22˝, for strap.

Lining fabric:
Cut 2 rectangles
13½˝ × 16½˝, for lining.

Cut 2 rectangles
8˝ × 9˝, for pocket.

Cut 2 strips 2˝ × 22˝, for strap.

Yellow accent fabric:
Cut 1 strip 4¼˝ × width of
fabric; subcut into 3 squares
4¼˝ × 4¼˝, and then cut each
square twice diagonally to make
12 quarter-square triangles.

Brown accent fabric:
Cut 1 strip 4¼˝ × width of
fabric; subcut into 3 squares
4¼˝ × 4¼˝, and then cut each
square twice diagonally to make
12 quarter-square triangles.

Continued on next page

Cutting, continued

Fusible batting:
Cut 2 rectangles 13½″ × 16½″, for tote body.

Fusible interfacing:
Cut 2 rectangles 13½″ × 16½″, for lining.

Cut 1 rectangle 8″ × 9″, for pocket.

Cut 4 strips 2″ × 22″, for strap.

Cut 2 squares 1½″ × 1½″, for snap reinforcement.

INSTRUCTIONS

Seam allowances are ¼″ for the patchwork front and ½″ for tote construction.

Zigzag patchwork

1. Use a ¼″ seam allowance to sew a linen triangle to a yellow accent triangle, right sides together, matching the short sides and offsetting the ends by ¼″. Press the seam gently to avoid stretching the fabrics.

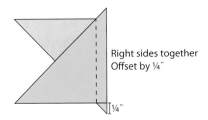

Right sides together
Offset by ¼″

¼″

2. Sew another linen triangle to the opposite side of the accent triangle in the same manner. Continue sewing, alternating between accent and linen triangles, until you have sewn 6 accent and 6 linen triangles.

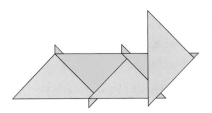

3. Repeat Steps 1 and 2 with the remaining yellow triangles and the 12 brown triangles to make 4 pieced triangle strips.

4. Sew the yellow strips together with the long sides of the triangles facing each other and the points offset to form the zigzag. Repeat for the brown accent fabric.

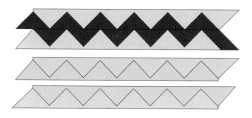

5. Sew the brown and yellow zigzag units together with the long sides of the linen triangles facing each other and the points offset. Trim to measure 16½″ × 6″.

Tote body

1. Sew the left front panel (5″ × 16½″) to the left side of the zigzag unit, and sew the right front panel (3½″ × 16½″) to the right side.

2. Fuse the batting to the pieced front and the 13½″ × 16½″ back rectangle, following the manufacturer's instructions.

3. Echo quilt the tote front ¼″ from the edges of the patchwork zigzag. Stitch 4 lines of quilting to the left of the yellow, 2 lines to the right of the brown, and 2 lines in between them. Then stitch another line 1″ away from each side. Quilt the tote back as desired.

4. Pin together the tote front and back, right sides facing, and then stitch around the sides and bottom, using a ½˝ seam allowance.

5. Pinch the bottom corners together, lining up the side and bottom seams. Use a ruler and pencil to draw a line measuring 3˝ from the point and perpendicular to the seam allowance. Pin and stitch, going slowly where the seam is thicker. Trim off the corner to ½˝. Repeat with the other corner. Turn the tote right side out and give it a good press all over.

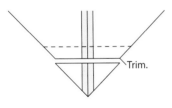

Trim.

Lining

1. Follow the manufacturer's instructions to fuse the 8˝ × 9˝ piece of interfacing to a pocket rectangle.

2. Pin and stitch the 2 pocket rectangles, right sides together, with a ¼˝ seam, leaving an opening on the bottom for turning.

3. Trim the corners and press a ¼˝ seam allowance in the bottom opening. Turn the pocket right side out, gently poke out the corners, and press. Set aside.

4. Fuse the 13½˝ × 16½˝ pieces of interfacing to the lining rectangles.

5. Measure and mark 1½˝ down from the top center on both lining pieces for the magnetic snap placement. Fuse the 1½˝ × 1½˝ interfacing squares at these marks, and then attach the snap parts here, following the manufacturer's directions.

6. Center the pocket on a lining piece; pin and stitch close to the side and bottom edges, backstitching at the beginning and end.

7. Pin and stitch the lining in the same manner as you did in Step 4 for the tote body, but leave an opening approximately 7˝ long in the center of the bottom seam for turning. Finger-press a ½˝ seam allowance in the opening.

8. Box the lining corners as in Step 5 for the tote body. Leave the lining wrong side out.

Straps

1. Fuse the 2″ × 22″ interfacing strips to the wrong sides of the 4 strap pieces.

2. Draw a line with a pencil down the long center of each strap piece.

3. Press the 2 long edges of each strip into the center, using lots of steam and the pencil line as a guide.

4. Place a lining strap onto a linen strap with the folded-in edges facing together; then topstitch ⅛″ in from each long edge. Repeat for the other 2 strap pieces.

5. Pin the straps to the top edge of the tote body, aligning the raw edges and positioning the straps 3½″ from the sides.

Tote assembly

1. Place the tote body inside the lining, right sides facing, with the straps sandwiched in between.

2. Match and pin the side seams first; then pin every couple of inches around the top edge.

3. Place the tote over the sewing machine's free arm and stitch all around the top edge using a ½″ seam, going slowly over the bulkier areas.

4. Pull the tote body out through the opening in the lining bottom.

5. Stitch the lining opening closed.

6. Push the lining into the tote body and press the top seam so the lining and the tote lie neat and flat against each other.

7. Topstitch ⅛″ or ¼″ around the top seam for a neat finish.

8. Give the whole tote a good pressing with steam.

The House Pouch

Little ones always want a place to keep their crayons and little treasures. Pretty lace detailing and sweet flower buttons make this pouch just the thing for kiddies of all ages.

FINISHED: 9″ × 8″

ARTIST: Julia Bravo

WEBSITE:
33stitches.blogspot.com

Julia has been crafting and sewing since she was a wee one. She spends her days creating all manner of pretty things for her online shops. When she is not sewing, Julia dabbles in experimental cooking, thrift store shopping, and her never-ending quest to learn to crochet. Born and raised in Southern California, she now lives along the Oregon Coast with her Mr. Wonderful, two Chihuahuas, and four fluffy cats.

Materials and Supplies

Linen or textured solid fabric: ¼ yard, for house front and back

Cotton print: ¼ yard, for roof

White fleece: scrap, at least 3″ × 6″ for window appliqués

Wood-grain print fabric: 4″ × 4″ scrap, for door appliqué

Gingham fabric: 1 fat quarter, for lining

Ruffled lace: 1 piece 20″ long

Lightweight fusible interfacing: ⅓ yard

Buttons for embellishment: 8 assorted

Zipper: 6″

Cutting

Linen:
Cut 2 rectangles 9½″ × 5″, for house.

Cotton print:
Cut 2 rectangles 9¾″ × 4″, for roof.

Gingham fabric:
Cut 2 rectangles 9½″ × 8½″, for lining.

Fusible interfacing:
Cut 2 rectangles 9½″ × 5″, for house.

Cut 2 rectangles 9¾″ × 4″, for roof.

Cut 2 rectangles 9½″ × 8½″, for lining.

INSTRUCTIONS

All seam allowances are ¼″. Templates are on page 114.

Appliquéing the house

1. Fuse interfacing to the wrong side of each linen rectangle, following the manufacturer's instructions.

2. Use the templates to cut out 1 door from the wood-grain fabric and 2 windows from the fleece.

3. Place the door at the bottom center of the house front and machine stitch in place with a zigzag or satin stitch. Attach a button for the doorknob.

4. Place a window on either side of the door and machine stitch in place as shown in the photo (page 14), stitching a center cross to create windowpanes.

5. Machine stitch 6 flower stems, 3 on either side of the door, leaving enough room to attach the button flowers.

6. Machine stitch 1 flower stem on the house back.

7. Attach the button flowers.

House and lining assembly

1. Fuse interfacing to the wrong side of the roof and lining rectangles.

2. Use the roof template to cut out both roof pieces.

3. Center align the top (the shorter side) of the roof template to the top edge of the lining rectangles. Mark the angled sides of the template and cut the lining along the marked lines. (Note: The base of the template is slightly wider than the lining.)

4. Center align and sew, right sides together, the long edge of a roof piece to the top edge of the house front. Press the seam open. Repeat for the back roof and house pieces.

5. Topstitch lace in place over the seams of both house pieces.

Final assembly

1. Attach the zipper to the top edge of the house front and lining pieces and sew the pouch together as described on page 17.

2. Give the pouch a final pressing, being careful to avoid the buttons.

ZIPPER TECHNIQUES

Follow these steps to attach a zipper to a pouch or wallet.

1. Sandwich the zipper between the top edge of an exterior and a lining piece. Align the raw edges with the zipper tape with right sides of the fabrics facing and the zipper pull facing the exterior. Pin the layers in place.

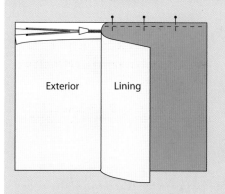

2. Use a zipper foot to stitch in place. Press the fabrics away from the zipper, wrong sides facing. Topstitch close to the zipper, if desired.

3. Repeat Steps 1 and 2 to sew the other side of the zipper tape to the remaining exterior and lining pieces.

4. Open the zipper about halfway; then align and pin the edges of the exterior pieces, right sides together. Align and pin the lining pieces, right sides together, matching up the zipper ends and making sure the teeth are facing down (to ensure a nice flush lining).

5. Start sewing at the lining bottom and stitch around all the sides, leaving a 3″ opening at the center bottom of the lining fabric.

6. Clip the ends of the zipper flush with the fabric layers. Trim the corners at an angle.

7. Pull the exterior right side out through the lining opening. With a pair of blunt scissors, carefully turn out the corners and zipper seams.

8. Machine or hand stitch the lining opening closed. Tuck the lining into the pouch.

Zakka Pincushion

FINISHED: 5½″ × 4¼″

Every sewer needs a pincushion in her sewing arsenal; this pretty one is designed in typical zakka style with crocheted lace, covered buttons, and stamping. You could even fill it with lavender for a special fragrant pick-me-up while you sew.

ARTIST: Sonia Cantié

WEBSITE:

cozyhomemaking.typepad.com

Sonia was born in southern France and currently lives in Montpellier with her husband and their two sons. A stay-at-home mom, she loves to freehand embroider, sew, take photos, paint with watercolors, dye with plants, bake, walk in nature, and collect all kinds of natural treasures. She also loves to repurpose all kinds of materials as often as she can and to create functional items with natural fibers almost exclusively.

Materials and Supplies

Natural linen or textured solid fabric: scrap, at least 3½″ × 5½″, for front

Pink linen or textured solid: scrap, at least 6½″ × 6¾″, for back

Cotton print: scrap, at least 4″ × 5¼″, for front

Fusible interfacing: scrap, at least 4″ × 5¼″, for front

½″-wide lace or rickrack: 5″

1 covered button: ½″ or ¾″ diameter, for front

1 button: ½″ or ¾″ diameter, for back

Polyester fiberfill

Optional for stamping:

Cream-colored cotton tape or muslin: 1¼″ wide × 2¼″ long

Small rubber stamp and textile ink pad

Iron for heat setting ink

Cutting

Natural linen:
Cut 1 rectangle 3″ × 4¾″, for front.

Pink linen:
Cut 1 rectangle 6″ × 4¾″, for back.

Cut 1 square 1½″ × 1½″, for button.

Cotton print:
Cut 1 rectangle 3½″ × 4¾″, for front.

Interfacing:
Cut 1 rectangle 3½″ × 4¾″, for front.

INSTRUCTIONS

All seam allowances are ¼˝.

Make the pincushion front

1. Fuse the interfacing to the cotton print, following the manufacturer's directions. Place the cotton print and the natural linen right sides together and sew along a long end (4¾˝). Press.

2. Pin the lace in place, close to the seam on the linen side of the pieced panel. Topstitch in place with matching thread.

3. *Optional:* Ink the rubber stamp and stamp the design centered onto the cotton tape. Allow the ink to dry (about a minute) and follow the manufacturer's instructions to heat set the ink with an iron (about 10 seconds). Fold in the raw ends of the stamped piece a bit and position it on the front panel as shown in photo (page 18). Topstitch in place around all the sides. Press the panel.

Assemble the pincushion

1. Align and pin the pink linen rectangle to the front panel, right sides together. Sew around all 4 sides, leaving a 2½˝ opening on a long side. Trim the corners at an angle. Turn the pincushion right side out and use a chopstick to push out the corners. Press flat, making sure to press in the seam allowance at the opening.

2. Stuff the pincushion evenly with polyester fiberfill, again using a chopstick to reach the corners. Hand sew the opening closed and rearrange the stuffing to remove lumps.

Add the buttons

1. Using the 1½″ × 1½″ square of pink linen, follow the manufacturer's instructions to cover the button.

2. Knot a needle and thread and then hand sew from the back through the pincushion to the front at the button placement point without threading the button. Return the needle to the back (but not through the same hole) and pull the thread gently to create a small dimple in the pincushion. Secure the threads with a knot, but do not cut the thread.

3. Return the needle to the front of the pincushion and through the shank of the linen-covered button. Then return the needle to the back and through the other button. Repeat to tighten the button placement. Knot to secure the buttons in place.

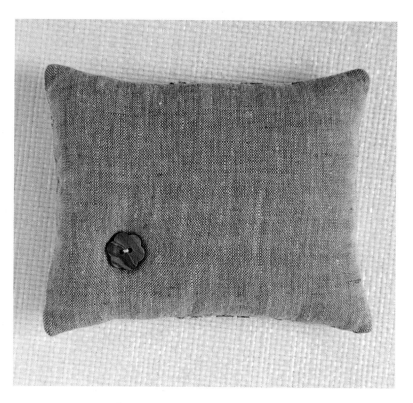

Sewing Kit

FINISHED: 7″ × 5″

We live in busy times, and crafting on the go is almost commonplace now. This sewing kit is perfect for bringing along your essential tools. It has a pincushion and pockets to hold everything from appliqué needles to scissors. Add a personal touch with a rubber stamp embellishment. Here, it's embellished with cute bird stamps.

ARTIST: Theresia Cookson

WEBSITE:

minoridesign.blogspot.com

Theresia has been creating soft toys and functional items from an early age. She loves to work with linen, woolen, and vintage fabrics to create her dolls. Although sewing is a passion, she also loves painting, cooking, blogging, and taking pictures with her Nikon DSLR camera. She gets most of her inspiration from vintage children's books, Japanese artists, and magazines. Theresia currently lives in Winchester, England, with her husband, two of her three grown-up children, and her old Burmese cat, Toby.

Materials and Supplies

Linen or textured solid fabric: ¼ yard, for pouch and pincushion

Print fabric: scrap, at least 10″ × 8″, for lining

Coordinating print fabric: scrap, at least 8½″ × 5¾″, for pincushion and binding

Lightweight cotton batting: scrap, at least 11″ × 8″

Water-soluble or chalk marker

2 brown leather thongs: 13″ long

Polyester fiberfill

Optional: Purchased rubber stamp (or rubber eraser and Speedball carving tool to make rubber stamp) and fabric ink

Cutting

Linen:

Cut 1 rectangle 10″ × 7½″, for pouch.

Cut 1 rectangle 6″ × 3¼″, for pincushion back.

Cut 1 square 3¼″ × 3¼″, for pincushion front.

Cut 2 rectangles 7½ ″ × 3″, for pockets.

Print fabric:

Cut 1 rectangle 10″ × 7½″, for lining.

Coordinating print fabric:

Cut 1 square 3¼″ × 3¼″, for pincushion front.

Cut 2 strips 8″ × 1″, for single-fold pocket binding.

Cotton batting:

Cut 1 rectangle 10″ × 7½″.

INSTRUCTIONS

All seam allowances are ¼″.

Pouch

1. Sew the binding strips to a long edge of each pocket piece, as if applying single-fold binding to a quilt (page 25), aligning the raw

edges and using a ¼″ seam allowance. Trim excess binding even with the pocket.

2. Topstitch the binding, by machine or hand, on the right side of the pocket close to the seam.

3. Measure and mark a line, with a water-soluble or chalk marker, 3″ in from each short edge of one pocket. See the diagram below.

4. Lay the pockets on either side of the lining, aligning the raw edges. Pin. Baste the pockets to the lining around the outside edges with a ⅛″ seam.

5. Make the pocket dividers by topstitching along the marked lines, back tacking at the binding edge.

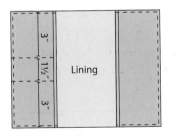

6. Place the pouch lining right side up. Position the leather thongs centered on the lining, with ½″ hanging over the edge of the divided pocket. Position the 10″ × 7½″ linen rectangle on top of the lining/pockets, right sides together, aligning the edges. Align the batting rectangle on the linen rectangle. Pin all the layers.

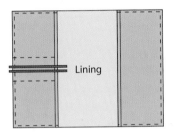

7. Stitch the layers together along all the sides, starting at a pocket edge and leaving a 2″ opening on the short end of the undivided pocket. Round the corners slightly while stitching, if desired.

8. Trim the corners, taking care to not cut the stitching, and turn the pouch right side out through the opening. Gently push out the corners and hand stitch the opening closed. Press flat. Add the optional rubber stamp embellishment.

Pincushion

1. Stitch together the 3¼″ × 3¼″ squares of linen and cotton fabric along one side. Add the optional rubber stamp embellishment (page 25).

2. Align the pieced top with the 6″ × 3¼″ back, right sides together. Sew along all the edges; leave a small opening for turning.

3. Trim the corners, and turn right side out through the opening. Press.

4. Stuff the pincushion with polyester fiberfill until firm (take care to not overstuff). Stitch the opening closed.

Optional embellishment

You can buy great handmade rubber stamps or make a stamp yourself by carving it from a rubber eraser using a Speedball carving tool. Choose a motif or print the name of the person who will be using the sewing pouch with alphabet stamps.

Do not forget to heat set the fabric ink with a hot iron to make the ink permanent.

BINDING TECHNIQUES

Single-fold binding

1. Pin the binding in place, aligning the raw edges, with right sides together. Sew the layers together using the designated seam allowance.

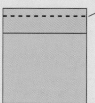

Sew using seam allowance indicated.

2. Press the binding up toward the seam and then fold it to the back, folding the raw edge under the same width as the seam allowance.

Press seam down.

Fold.

Press seam up.

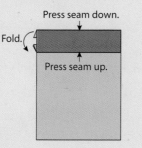

3. Hand stitch the binding to the back.

Fold under and stitch.

Double-fold binding

1. Fold the binding strip in half lengthwise, with wrong sides together.

2. Pin the binding in place on the front side of the fabric, aligning the raw edges. Sew the layers together using the designated seam allowance.

3. Fold the binding strip to the back and hand stitch to the back.

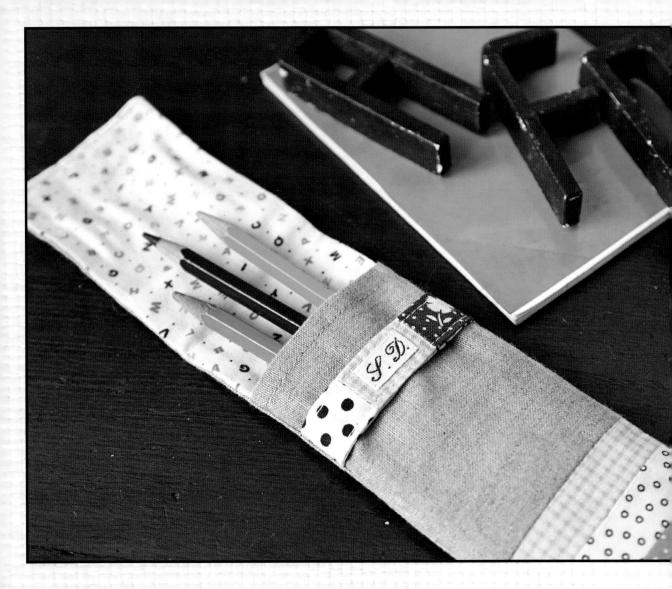

Patchwork Pencil Case

This simple patchwork case is a charming design for holding pens, pencils, crochet needles—whatever you like! To personalize the case, add embellishments such as embroidery or vintage buttons. Here, a monogram was machine embroidered on twill tape and stitched in place.

FINISHED: approximately 2½″ × 6¾″

ARTIST: Shannon Dréval

WEBSITE: petitsdetails.com

Shannon grew up in the United States and now lives a short walk from Paris with her husband and son. Since moving to France ten years ago—and thanks in large part to a wonderful online community—she has come to love sewing, cross-stitching, and making things in general. Her blog, "Petits Détails," also began several years ago. The name is French for "little details." She notes the unique and endearing qualities of hand-made items, the small features or signs of age that add beauty and character to vintage objects, and the little facts and features of everyday life in France.

Materials and Supplies

Linen or textured solid fabric: ¼ yard*

Lining fabric: ¼ yard

Lightweight fusible interfacing: ¼ yard

Assorted prints: scraps, for patchwork stripes and closing band

Optional: Button and/or small bits of ribbon or trim, for embellishment

A tightly woven, relatively light-weight linen works best, since this is a small project.

Cutting

Linen:
Cut 1 piece 3″ × 3¾″.

Cut 1 piece 3″ × 11¾″.

Lining fabric:
Cut 1 piece 3″ × 16½″.

Lightweight fusible interfacing:
Cut 1 piece 2½″ × 16″.

Assorted print scraps:
Cut 3 pieces 1½″ × 2½″, for closing band.

Cut 3 pieces 1″ × 3″, for patchwork stripes.

INSTRUCTIONS

All seam allowances are ¼″. A walking foot may be helpful when top-stitching the closing band and assembling the case.

Closing band and patchwork stripes

I've added a vintage monogrammed ribbon to the band, but you could add any embellishment you like to it—a button or trim, for example.

1. Sew the 3 closing band 1½″ × 2½″ pieces together along the 2½″ sides to make a 2½″ × 3½″ strip set.

2. Fold the strip set in half lengthwise (3½″ length), wrong sides together. Press.

3. Unfold; then fold in the long edges so they meet at the center crease. Press.

4. Refold the piece along the original center crease; press and pin to keep it from opening.

5. Trim the strip to measure 3″ long.

6. Topstitch the strip ⅛″ or so from each long edge to finish the closing band. Set aside.

7. Sew the 3 patchwork stripe 1″ × 3″ pieces together along the 3″ sides to make a 3″ × 2″ strip set. Press the seams open. Set aside.

Pencil case assembly

1. Align the 3″ edges and sew the 3″ × 3¾″ linen piece to the top edge of the patchwork stripes and the 3″ × 11¾″ linen piece to the bottom edge. Press the seams open.

2. Place the closing band 1″ down from the top edge of the smaller piece of linen, and machine baste each side ⅛″ in from the edge so that the stitching won't appear once the case is sewn together.

3. Center the fusible interfacing on the wrong side of the lining piece and fuse, following the manufacturer's instructions.

4. Align the lining on the assembled patchwork exterior, right sides together. Sew across the 3″ edge of the smaller piece of linen. Press the seam open.

5. Fold the lining back along the seam just sewn, so that the lining and the exterior are aligned along all the edges, wrong sides together. Press.

6. Topstitch on the linen side, ⅛″ to ¼″ from the fold.

7. Place the piece, lining side up, on the ironing surface, keeping the lining and exterior aligned with wrong sides together. Measure and fold the lining,

right sides together, 5½″ from the topstitched edge. Press. Turn the piece over and fold the exterior in the same manner, aligning the raw and folded edges. Press.

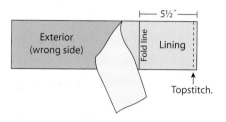

8. Sew around the 3 raw edges, leaving an opening of about 1¼″ in the center of the 3″ end. Press the seams open. Trim the corners.

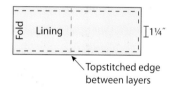

9. Turn the piece right side out through the opening (a chopstick or knitting needle can come in handy here). Press.

10. Turn under the seam allowance on the opening and topstitch ⅛″ or so from the edge to close it.

Voilà, you're finished!

Itty Bitty Quilt Block Magnets

Made to resemble traditional quilt blocks, these little cuties may be "itty bitty," but they are huge on zakka style! Make one block or make all six for a coordinated display on your fridge or magnetic board.

FINISHED: 1½˝ × 1½˝

ARTIST: Nova Flitter

WEBSITE:

acuppaandacatchup.com

Nova has always been a little bit crafty, cutting and gluing and sewing since she can remember. Her real passion for sewing was sparked about ten years ago, after she and her husband emigrated to Australia from the United Kingdom and she bought her first very own sewing machine. With a sewing machine in the house 24/7, she just wanted to sew, sew, sew! Nova loves to sew all sorts of stuff, from quilts to small projects like pillows, bags, home goods, and clothing. She can often be found in her pajamas, with a cuppa (tea) by her side and a needle and thread in her hand, doing what she loves best. She's passionate about the online quilting and craft community, participating in swaps and virtual bees.

Materials and Supplies

Makes 6 magnets.

Linen or textured solid fabric: assorted scraps, for blocks

Small-print cotton quilting fabric: assorted scraps, for blocks

Contrasting quilting cotton: 1 scrap at least 6″ × 4″, for backs*

Lightweight batting or fusible fleece: 1 piece at least 9″ × 6″

Embroidery floss

Magnetic sheet: 8½″ × 11″**

2″ × 2″ square of paper, for string block

Gluestick

Dark colors work better because the magnet won't show through.

**Available at art suppliers or from printers who use them for magnetic business cards*

Cutting

For each magnet block, cut the following:

From contrasting quilting cotton: 1 square 2″ × 2″

From batting or fusible fleece: 1 square 3″ × 3″

From magnetic sheet: 2 squares 1⅜″ × 1⅜″

For quilt block cutting instructions, see instructions for individual blocks.

INSTRUCTIONS

All seam allowances are ¼″. Trim to ⅛″ after pressing to reduce bulk. Set your stitch length to smaller than normal (about 1.5).

Block assembly

Nine Patch

1. Cut 5 squares of linen 1″ × 1″ and 4 squares of printed fabric 1″ × 1″.

2. Arrange and sew the squares together as shown to form a Nine Patch. Press the seams in alternate directions; trim the seam allowances to ⅛″.

Pinwheel

1. Cut 2 squares of linen 1⅝″ × 1⅝″ and 2 squares of print fabric 1⅝″ × 1⅝″.

2. Make half-square triangle units by placing the linen squares and printed squares right sides together. Use a pencil and ruler to draw a line diagonally across the square and sew ¼″ along each side of the line. Cut along the pencil line and press all the seams toward the linen. Trim the seam allowances to ⅛″ and trim off the dog-ears.

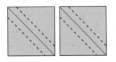

3. Arrange the squares as shown and sew them together. Press the seams in alternate directions; trim the seam allowances to ⅛″.

Offset Log Cabin

1. Cut 1 square of linen 1″ × 1″ (A). From a print fabric (B), cut 1 square 1″ × 1″ and 1 rectangle 1″ × 1½″, and from another print (C), cut 1 rectangle 1″ × 1½″ and 1 rectangle 2″ × 1″.

2. Sew the units in order, pressing and trimming each seam allowance to ⅛″, as follows:

Sew the 1″ × 1″ print (A) square to the 1″ × 1″ linen (B) square.

Add the 1″ × 1½″ rectangle (B) as shown.

Add the 1″ × 1½″ rectangle (C) as shown.

Add the 2″ × 1″ rectangle (C) along the bottom to complete the Log Cabin.

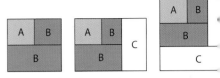

Friendship Star

1. Cut 1 square 1″ × 1″ of print fabric (A) for the star center. Cut 1 square 1⅜″ × 1⅜″ *each* from another print (B) and from a third print (C). Cut 4 squares of linen 1″ × 1″ and 2 squares of linen 1⅜″ × 1⅜″.

2. Use the linen, (B), and (C) 1⅜″ × 1⅜″ squares to make 4 half-square triangle units (see Pinwheel, Step 2).

3. Arrange and sew together the (A) center square, the 4 linen 1″ squares, and the 4 half-square triangles. Press the seams in alternate directions; trim the seam allowances to ⅛″.

Brick Cross

1. Cut 4 rectangles of linen 1¼″ × ⅞″. Cut 2 rectangles 1¼″ × ⅞″ from print (A) and 2 more from another print (B).

2. Place the linen and the print rectangles right sides together and chain piece. Press and trim the seam allowances to ⅛″.

3. Arrange the squares as shown and sew together. Press the seams in alternate directions; trim the seam allowances to ⅛″.

String

1. Cut 1 rectangle of linen 1¼″ × 3″. Cut 2 rectangles 1″ × 2½″ from a print (A). Cut 2 rectangles 1″ × 1¾″ from another print (B).

2. Center the linen rectangle diagonally across a 2″ × 2″ square of paper. Secure it with a tiny dab of glue. Lay a fabric A rectangle on top of the linen strip, right sides together and aligning the edges. Sew together along the aligned edge and finger-press open. Repeat on the other side. Then repeat with fabric B. Press.

You'll end up with an odd-shaped block like this.

3. Flip it over and trim it even with the paper square. Carefully tear the paper away. Trim the seam allowances to ⅛″.

Magnet assembly

1. Place a 3″ × 3″ square of batting or fusible fleece (follow the manufacturer's directions) under the quilt block. Using sewing thread or 2 strands of embroidery thread, quilt the block as desired with running stitches. Trim off the excess batting.

2. Align a 2″ × 2″ square of contrasting fabric on the quilted block, right sides together. Sew around 3 sides of the block, backstitching at the start and finish. You may find it easiest to sew with the batting side up to avoid catching the batting on the feed dogs.

3. Carefully trim the seam allowances to ⅛″ and clip the 2 sewn corners at an angle. Trim away excess batting right up to the seam, being careful not to snip the seam!

4. Turn the block right side out. Use a small knitting needle or chopstick to help, but be gentle because the seams are tiny. Press.

5. Slide 2 magnet squares into the open end. Check that both magnetic sides are facing the back! Turn under the seam allowances at the opening and slipstitch closed (tiny appliqué pins are really helpful at this stage).

Voilà! One little sampler quilt!

Rain Cloud Mug Rug

This cute little mug rug with its lovely appliquéd cloud will brighten anyone's day, rain or shine. Embellished with hand embroidery and a touch of machine quilting, this tiny quilt is simple to make. Stitch up a few to make a complete set!

FINISHED: *7″ × 7″*

ARTIST: Christie Fowler

WEBSITE: www.pigeon-pair.com

Christie lives in Melbourne, Australia, with her husband and two kids. She loves to sew, knit, quilt, and stitch, and she loves to learn new crafts. She keeps a record of her crafts at her blog. Visit her there!

Materials and Supplies

Sky-blue linen or textured solid fabric: 8″ × 8″ square, or larger, for background

Polka dot fabric: ¼ yard, for backing and binding

White fabric: small scrap, at least 3½″ × 2″, for cloud appliqué

Batting: 9″ × 9″

Embroidery floss: gray and light gray

Water-soluble fabric marker

Basting spray

Cutting

Template is on page 114.

Linen:
Cut 1 square 8″ × 8″.

Polka dot fabric:
Cut 1 square 8″ × 8″, for backing.

Cut 2 strips 1½″ × remaining-width-of-fabric, for single-fold binding.

INSTRUCTIONS

All seam allowances are ¼″.

Appliqué

1. Use a water-soluble marker and the template to trace the cloud shape onto the white fabric. Cut around the shape, leaving a ¼″ seam allowance.

2. Center the white cloud shape on the linen square and use 1 or 2 pins to hold it in place. Starting at any point, fold under the seam allowance, so that you can just see the marked line, and needle-turn hand appliqué the cloud onto the linen. Wet the marker lines to remove them before pressing.

Embellishments

1. Use the template to mark "wind" and "rain" lines on the appliquéd linen, or stitch without marking.

2. Layer and baste the appliquéd square and batting (the backing will be added later).

3. Machine or hand quilt the "wind" lines.

4. Use one strand of embroidery floss and small running stitches to create "rain" lines, alternating between the 2 shades of gray.

Assembly

1. Use basting spray to attach the backing fabric.

2. Measure and trim the quilt to 7″ × 7″ square, ensuring that the cloud is centered.

3. Bind the quilt using a ¼″ seam allowance. See Single-fold Binding, (page 25).

Zakka Block Quilt

FINISHED: 45″ × 61″

Spring, summer, fall, or winter—this simple lap quilt will be a welcome addition to any cozy home all year round. The bold cotton print One Patch blocks and linen sashing are quick and easy to put together. Hand or machine quilt this project in any way you like to add your own special style.

ARTIST: Leslie Good

WEBSITE: goodness.typepad.com

Leslie has always had a creative streak and is constantly adding to her list of new things to try. She inherited her mother's love for fabric and sewing, and this is definitely her favorite creative outlet. Living in Japan for five years helped fuel her fabric addiction, and she started quilting a few years ago. When she moved back to Canada, she brought enough Japanese fabric (25 boxes!) to last for years, and she always has a few quilts in progress.

Materials and Supplies

Cotton prints: a variety totaling 1 yard, for blocks*

Linen or textured solid fabric: 2⅝ yards, for blocks, sashing, backing, and binding

Blue print fabric: ⅔ yard, for backing

White print fabric: 1¾ yards, for backing

Batting: 49″ × 65″

Some backing prints were used for blocks.

Cutting

Cotton prints:

Cut 30 squares 6″ × 6″ from a variety of fabrics, for blocks.

Linen:

Cut the strips in order as follows:

Cut 3 strips 6″ × width of fabric; subcut into 24 rectangles 6″ × 4¾″, for short sashing between blocks.

Cut 6 strips 2½″ × width of fabric, for double-fold binding.

From the remaining length of fabric:

Cut 5 strips 6″ × *length* of fabric, for long sashing between rows.

Cut 1 strip 9½″ × *length* of fabric; trim to 9½″ × 56″, for backing.

Blue print:

Cut 1 strip 9½″ × width of fabric; trim to 9½″ × 40″, for backing.

Cut 1 square 9½″ × 9½″, for backing.

White print:

Cut 1 rectangle 40″ × 56″, for backing.

INSTRUCTIONS

All seam allowances are ¼˝.

Quilt top

1. Refer to the diagram below to arrange the print squares and linen rectangles into 6 rows on the design wall, placing the long linen sashing strips between the rows.

2. Sew the 6 rows together. Press the seams.

3. Measure the sewn rows and cut the long sashing to this length (approx. 45˝). Sew the linen sashing strips between the rows. Press the seams toward the sashing.

4. Square up the quilt top to 45˝ × 61˝.

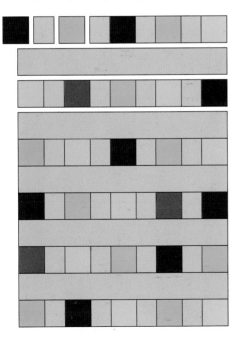

Quilt back

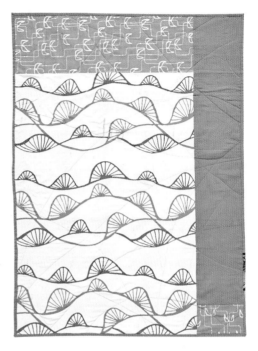

1. Sew the small blue print 9½˝ × 9½˝ square to the end of the linen 9½˝ × 56˝ rectangle. Press the seam.

2. Sew the large blue 9½˝ × 40˝ strip to the end of the white print 40˝ × 56˝ rectangle. Press the seam.

3. Sew the 2 pieced backing strips together (see the photo, above). Press the seam.

Quilting and finishing

1. Layer, baste, and quilt as desired.

2. Bind the quilt using your preferred binding method or refer to Double-fold Binding (page 25).

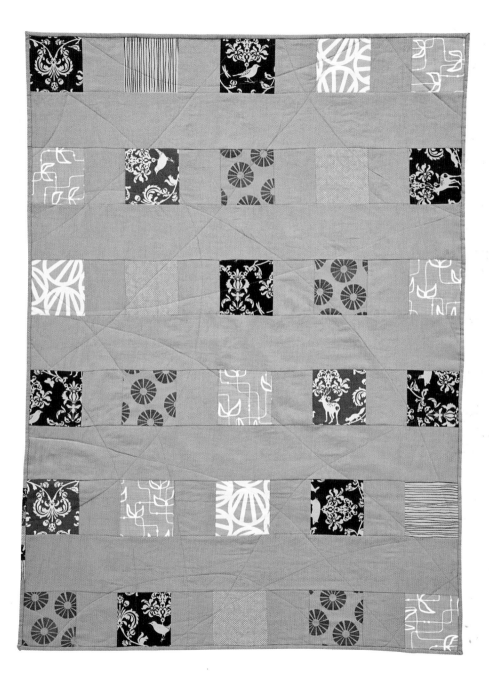

Stem Messenger Bag

FINISHED: 13″ wide × 11″ high × 3″ deep (excluding the strap)

A bold, colorful appliquéd stem of leaves adds to the appeal of this practical messenger bag. It features a sturdy adjustable strap along with lots of pockets and space for holding your phone, a laptop, even that new knitting project you just started!

ARTIST: Larissa Holland

WEBSITE:

mmmcrafts.blogspot.com

Larissa has loved to craft and draw ever since she can remember. Growing up, she was lucky to be surrounded by clever, creative women in her family and credits her grand-mothers, mom, and sisters for her appreciation of and joy in handmade things. She has been inspired by the renewed interest in handcrafting and the zakka style in particular. Now that her career as a graphic designer has become one of full-time mom and homeschool teacher, she craves the creative outlet that sewing and paper crafts provide. Designing and making everyday items that have beauty and meaning bring her a lot of cre-ative satisfaction, and she enjoys giving them as gifts to her family and friends. Nothing says love like handmade.

Materials and Supplies

Yardage is based on 45″-wide fabric, unless otherwise noted.

Natural linen or textured solid: 1 yard, for bag body

Coordinating fabric: 1⅓ yards, for lining

Various solid and shot cottons*: 12 scraps, at least 3″ × 7″, for patchwork leaves

Brown fabric (or heavyweight canvas**): ⅓ yard, at least 54″ wide, for strap

1 package ½″ brown double-fold bias binding, for stem and trim

Fusible web (such as HeatnBond by Therm O Web): ½ yard

Medium-weight fusible inter-facing (such as Décor-Bond by Pellon): ½ yard, for bag body and flap, plus 1⅛ yards, for straps**

1 metal tri-bar slider and rect-angular loop combo: 1½″, for adjustable strap (available from sewingsupplies.etsy.com)

Linen-colored or coordinating thread, for topstitching and appliqué

Washable fabric glue

Air-soluble fabric marker

*Shot cotton is specially woven with one color of thread for the weft and a different color for the warp. This weaving process cre-ates subtle changes in the fabric's color as it moves and light hits it.

**If you use a heavyweight canvas fabric for the strap, you won't have to back it with fusible interfacing.

Cutting

Templates are on pages 115 and 116.

Body of bag:
Cut 1 rectangle 14″ × 25″ *each* from linen, lining fabric, and fusible interfacing.

Outside/inside pocket:
Cut 1 rectangle 14″ × 18″ from linen.

Cut 3 rectangles 14″ × 18″ from lining fabric.

Flap:
Cut 1 rectangle 12″ × 13½″ *each* from linen, lining fabric, and fusible interfacing.

Strap:
Cut 1 rectangle 4″ × 54″ *each* from strap fabric and fusible interfacing.*

Cut 1 rectangle 4″ × 8″ each from strap fabric and fusible interfacing.*

Patchwork leaves:
Cut 12 rectangles 3″ × 7″ from various cotton fabrics.

*If you use a heavyweight canvas fabric for the strap, you won't have to back it with fusible interfacing.

INSTRUCTIONS

All seam allowances are ¼″.

Assembling the body/pocket

1. Iron the fusible interfacing to the back of the linen bag body, following the manufacturer's instructions.

2. Align the linen 14″ × 18″ pocket rectangle with a lining pocket rectangle, right sides together. Sew the short sides of the pocket (14″), leaving the long sides unsewn. Turn right side out and press. Topstitch ⅛″ away from the sewn edges. Repeat with the 2 remaining lining pocket rectangles.

3. Lay the linen pocket piece (linen side out) on the right side of the linen body piece, centered from top to bottom. Pin and baste together on the long edges of the pocket. Using an air-soluble marker, draw a center line; then draw the remaining guidelines, as shown. Topstitch with linen-colored thread across the guidelines.

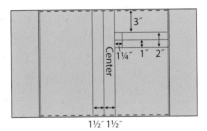

4. Repeat Step 3 for the lining body and pocket, drawing the guidelines, then topstitching them, as shown.

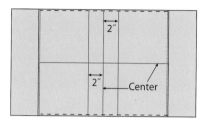

Making the leaves

1. Align and pin 2 contrasting 3″ × 7″ leaf rectangles, right sides together. Sew along a long edge and press the seam allowance open. Follow the manufacturer's instructions to apply fusible web to the wrong side of the assembled piece. Peel off the backing. Repeat with the other leaf rectangles for a total of 6 leaves.

2. Use an air-soluble marker to trace the leaf template on the right side of the 6 patchwork pieces, aligning the center line of the template with the seam. Carefully cut out the leaves. Set aside.

Making the bag flap

1. Iron the fusible interfacing to the back of the linen flap, following the manufacturer's instructions.

2. Align and trace, with an air-soluble marker, the curved corner template (page 116) on each bottom corner of the linen and lining flap pieces. Trim to create the curved corners.

3. Press a 15″ piece of bias binding to make it nice and flat. Use dots of fabric glue to tack it down along the center of the bag flap (see page 46). After the glue is dry (I help this along with my iron), topstitch $1/16$″ away from both long edges with linen-colored thread. Trim off the extra.

4. Draw leaf placement guide-lines on the flap as shown. Following the instructions on the fusible web, carefully fuse the leaves in place one at a time, making sure they are aligned with the guides. Trim the overhanging leaves flush with the top edge. Using a zigzag or satin stitch, sew around the edge of each leaf with linen-colored thread.

5. Align and pin the linen and lining flap pieces, right sides together. Sew around the 2 sides and curved bottom, leaving the top open for turning. Notch the curved edges every ½″ or more so they lie smooth after turning.

6. Turn the flap right side out and press the edges. Pin and topstitch ⅛″ away from the finished edges, using linen-colored thread. Pin and baste the top (open) edge. Follow the package directions to attach double-fold binding to the top (basted) edge, folding the ends under for a finished look.

Assembling the bag

1. Lay the top edge of the flap, right side up, on the right side of the linen body piece (on the end without the pencil slots). Center the flap from side to side and about 2″ below the short edge. Topstitch ¹⁄₁₆″ away from both edges of the bias binding, backstitching at each end to reinforce the seam.

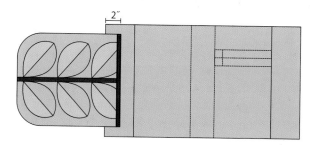

2. Fold the body piece in half, right sides together, with the flap tucked inside and out of the way. Pin and sew up both sides.

3. Pinch the bottom corners together, lining up the side and bottom seams. Use a ruler and pencil to draw a line measuring 3″ from the point and perpendicular to the seam allowance. Pin and stitch, going slowly where the seam is thicker. Trim off the corner to ½″. Repeat with the other corner.

4. Repeat Steps 2 and 3 for the lining pieces.

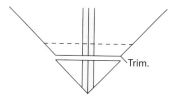

Making and attaching the adjustable strap

1. If applicable, iron the fusible interfacing to the back of the strap pieces, following the manufacturer's instructions.

2. Press under ½″ on each long edge of the 4″ × 54″ strap piece. Press under ½″ on a short end. Press the whole strap in half lengthwise, wrong sides together, aligning the folded edges. The strap should now measure 1½″ × 53½″. Pin and topstitch ⅛″ away from the folded-under edges.

3. Repeat Step 2 for the 4″ × 8″ strap piece, except leave both ends raw. The strap should measure 1½″ × 8″.

4. Feed the short strap through the 1½″ metal rectangular loop and fold it in half. Sew across the strap near the loop to secure the loop inside the strap. Trim off the raw edges of the strap so that the fabric part is about 3″ long.

5. From underneath, feed the finished end of the long strap around the center bar of the tri-bar slider, overlapping it on itself by 2″. Pin and sew around the edges to form a rectangle with a cross inside to secure the 2″ tab in place.

6. Feed the raw end of the long strap through the underside of the rectangular loop and then under the first bar of the tri-bar slider, over the center bar, and under the third bar, as shown. Continue feeding it through so that most of the strap goes through the bars.

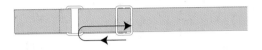

7. Pin the raw edges of the assembled adjustable strap, with the wrong side facing out, to the right side of the linen bag body, as shown. Leave ½˝ hanging over the raw edges, and center the strap with the side seams. Baste in place. Adjust the strap to a shorter length to make the next step easier.

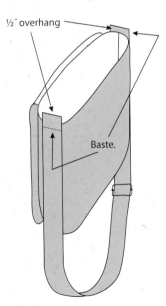

½˝ overhang

Baste.

Finishing

1. Turn the lining wrong side out and the body right side out. Stuff the body/flap/strap inside the lining, right sides facing. The flap and strap will be stuffed down in between the 2 layers; tuck them in and smooth them down so they stay out of the way. Pin the body and lining together around the top, aligning the side seams and raw edges (the strap ends will be sticking up). I recommend hand basting the body and lining together before the next step.

2. Carefully sew around the raw edges of the opening, reinforcing the straps with backstitching and leaving about 6˝ open in the center of the flap side for turning. Make sure to backstitch well at the beginning and end; turning this stiff fabric puts a lot of stress on the stitches. Turn the bag right side out through the opening and then stuff the lining inside the bag.

3. Press the seam around the top, rolling it between your fingers to get it as close to the stitching as possible. Press under the seam allowance on the opening. Pin and topstitch ⅛˝ away from the edge all the way around the top of the bag.

4. Press any wrinkles left in the bag from turning.

Zip Organizer

FINISHED: 5½″ × 8″

This pretty and useful project offers lots of pockets, with space for business cards, your ID, and plenty more to help you stay organized while on the go. There's even a place for your pen. The neat zipper closure keeps all your goodies nice and secure.

ARTIST: Masko Jefferson

WEBSITE: siamsquare.etsy.com

Before finding her inner crafty, Masko found her thrills in the great outdoors as a beach girl, island hopper, world traveler, and scuba diver. When her children were born, she had to find an alternate hobby that would keep her inside the house. A handmade quilt that a friend gave her sparked the beginning of her life as a creator. After sewing for eight years, she started her tiny sewing business, Siam Square, on Etsy in 2007, and she has since expanded her creativity from quilting to bag making. She loves challenges and developing new things, and often when she sees a purse or wallet at the store, her mind kicks into overdrive trying to figure out how it was made. Her home country of Japan is full of inspiration, and she always looks forward to her next visit.

Materials and Supplies

Linen, linen/cotton blend, or cotton (prints and solids): ⅓ yard each of 3 different fabrics, for inner and outer panels, pockets, and pen holder*

Contrasting print: ½ yard, for lining, bias tape, and zipper end tab

Canvas, quilt batting, or other heavy material: 3½″ × 8″, for inner reinforcement

Medium-weight fusible interfacing: ⅓ yard

Lightweight fusible interfacing: ½ yard

7″ zipper

20″ zipper

The fabric used for the outer panel is printed to look like patchwork.

Cutting

Linen:
Cut 1 rectangle 11″ × 8″, for outer panel.

Cut 1 rectangle 11″ × 8″, for inner panel.

Cut 1 rectangle 3¾″ × 8″ from each of 3 prints, for 3 card pockets.

From the remaining fabric, cut the pockets as follows (Note: Each pocket is cut from a different fabric.):
Cut 1 rectangle 5¼″ × 8″, for large pocket.

Cut 1 rectangle 4¾″ × 8″, for medium passport pocket.

Cut 1 rectangle 4¼″ × 8″, for small checkbook pocket.

From the leftover fabric:
Cut 1 rectangle 3½″ × 2″, for pen holder.

Contrasting print:
Cut 2 rectangles 11″ × 8″, for lining.

Cut 1 square 12″ × 12″, for bias binding.

Cut 1 rectangle 3½″ × 2, for zipper tab.

Continued on next page

**Medium-weight
fusible interfacing:**

Cut 2 rectangles 11˝ × 18˝,
for outer and inner panels.

Lightweight fusible interfacing:

Cut 3 rectangles 3¾˝ × 8˝.

Cut 1 rectangle 5¼˝ × 8˝.

Cut 1 rectangle 4¾˝ × 8˝.

Cut 1 rectangle 4¼˝ × 8˝.

INSTRUCTIONS

All seam allowances are ¼˝, unless otherwise noted.

Apply interfacing

1. Fuse medium-weight interfacing to the wrong side of the outer and inner panel pieces, following the manufacturer's instructions.

2. Fuse lightweight interfacing to the wrong side of all 6 pocket pieces.

Finish the pocket edges

The inside of the organizer contains pockets that are stacked one on top of the other in a staggered fashion (see the photo below). The right inner panel pockets are stacked from largest (in the back) to smallest (on top). For the card pockets on the left inner panel, the fabrics and stacking order should match the fabrics of the right inner panel.

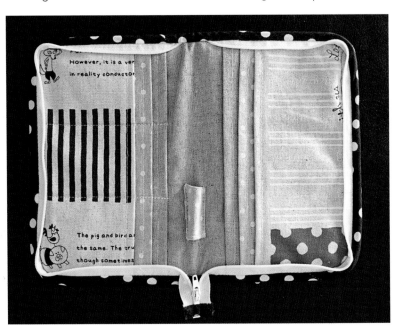

1. Card pockets (left inner panel): For the top-layer card pocket, zigzag or serge finish along 1 long edge. For all the other card pockets, zigzag or serge finish both long edges.

2. Large, medium (passport), and small (checkbook) pockets (right inner panel): Zigzag or serge finish only 1 long side.

3. All pockets: Fold one long zigzag-finished edge of each pocket under ½″ toward the wrong side of the fabric and press. Topstitch with a ¼″ seam.

Make the inner panel

1. Using the edge of a cup or other round object to mark the curves to trim, round all 4 corners of the 11″ × 8″ inner panel.

2. Fold the inner panel in half lengthwise, along the long (11″) edge, and mark the center at both the top and bottom. Measure ¾″ from each side of the center and mark at the top and bottom. Then, measure ⅝″ from each side of the center and mark at the top and bottom.

3. Center the 3½″ × 8″ canvas on the wrong side of the inner panel, aligning the top and bottom edges. Pin and sew the canvas in place (the stitches will be hidden under the pocket pieces). The canvas will support the center where there are fewer layers.

4. Fold the 3½″ × 2″ pen holder piece in half lengthwise, right sides together. Sew the folded fabric around the 3 raw edges, leaving a 1″ opening. Turn right side out, tuck the seam inside the opening, and press. Topstitch the sides of the pen holder to the

center of the inner panel, with each side approximately ¼″ away from the center line (see the photo, page 52).

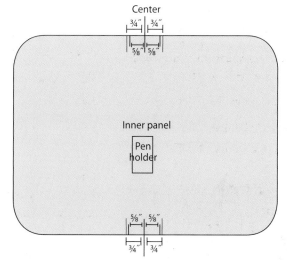

Left Inner Panel

1. With the pocket right side up, align the bottom card pocket's hemmed edge with the ¾″ top and bottom marks on the left side of the inner panel. Pin and sew ¼″ from the pocket's long raw edge.

2. Place the next card pocket on the previous pocket, right sides up and aligning the hemmed edge ¾″ away from the previous pocket's hemmed edge. Pin and sew ¼″ from the long raw edge. Repeat for the third (top) card pocket.

3. Trim the pocket corners using the inner panel as a guide to create the curves.

4. Baste the pockets to the inner panel, close to the edge, along the short raw edges.

5. Mark and topstitch 2 lines 2¾˝ from both the top and bottom edges to divide the card pockets into 3 sections, as shown. There will be 9 card slots in total.

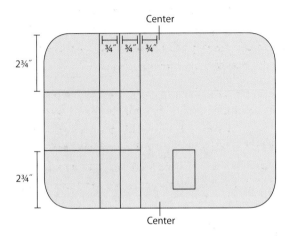

Center

¾˝ ¾˝ ¾˝

2¾˝

2¾˝

Center

Right Inner Panel

1. With the pocket right side up, align the large pocket's hemmed edge with the ¾˝ top and bottom marks on the right side of the inner panel. Position the medium and small pockets on top, aligning the raw edges. Pin.

2. Trim the pocket corners using the inner panel as a guide to create the curves.

3. Pin and baste the pockets to the lining, close to the edge, along the raw edges.

Make the outer panel

1. Measure and cut a 3¾˝ separated pocket piece from the short end of the 11˝ × 8˝ outer panel and one lining rectangle to create 2 pieces, 1 from each fabric; they will measure 3¾˝ × 8˝ and 7¼˝ × 8˝.

2. Align the 7˝ zipper to the just-cut edge of the separated pocket lining piece (3¾˝ × 8˝), right sides together. Sew the zipper to the lining following Steps 1 and 2 of Zipper Techniques (page 17). Repeat for the other side (7¼˝ × 8˝) of the cut lining and outer panel.

3. Baste the layers together about ⅛˝ from the edge to finish the outer panel.

4. Place the finished outer panel, right side up, on top of the remaining 11˝ × 8˝ lining piece (the lining fabric will be right sides together). Align and pin the raw edges of all 3 fabric layers. Baste ⅛˝ around all the raw edges to hold the layers in place.

5. Cut off the excess zipper ends, if any.

Join the panels

1. Align and pin the inner and outer panels, wrong sides together. Trim the corners of the outer panel to match the curves of the inner panel. Baste the layers together about ⅛˝ from all the edges.

2. Mark the 20˝ zipper 2˝ from the closed end on each side of the zipper tape, right side up (the side with the zipper pull). Unzip the zipper all the way. Match the 2˝ marks on the zipper with the ⅝˝ marks on the bottom edge of the inner panel. Pin.

3. Refer to the photo below and pin the zipper tape along each side of the inner panel, aligning the edges of the tape with the raw edges of the panel. Make small clips in the zipper tape along the curved corners to help ease the zipper in place. Angle the zipper off the edge at each ⅝″ mark at the top of the inner panel. The zipper ends will be tucked into the binding later.

4. Use a zipper foot, starting at the bottom edge of the panel, to sew the zipper to each side of the panel about ¼″ from the edges. Cut off the excess zipper at the top of the panel.

Bind and finish

1. Fold under the tail ends of the zipper tape at the closed end of the zipper. Pin.

2. Make bias tape from the 12″ × 12″ square of contrasting fabric. Cut the square in half on the diagonal (45°) and then cut 1½″ strips along the angle. Sew the strips end to end on a diagonal to make at least 52″ of bias tape.

3. Sew the bias tape to the outside edges of the organizer as if applying single-fold binding to a quilt, aligning the raw edges and using a ¼″ seam allowance. (See Single-fold Binding, page 25).

4. Use the 3½″ × 2″ contrasting print rectangle to make a zipper tab in the same manner as the pen holder (Step 4, page 53). Fold the tab over the folded ends of the zipper tail. Pin and topstitch to secure the zipper inside the tab. Make sure the zipper pull is out of the way so you don't sew over it.

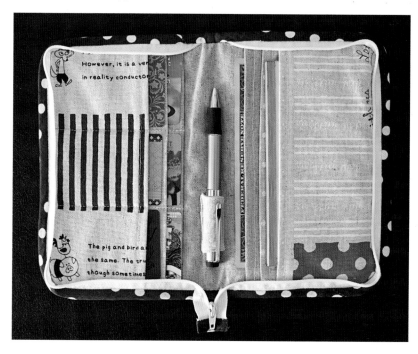

Orchard Path
Tweed Pouch

Tweed has such a lovely texture, and it's used brilliantly in this pouch project. With hexagon goodness and stylish corner details, how can you resist? Fill it with all your essentials and toss it in that new tote you just made!

FINISHED: 9½″ × 6¾″

ARTIST: Amanda Jennings

WEBSITE:

msmcporkchopquilts.com

Amanda is the quilter behind msmcporkchopquilts.com. She's a wife to the greatest Porkchop in the world, a lover of all things Japanese, an obsessive linen buyer, and a candy cane aficionado. When she's not sewing up a storm, she's in the kitchen baking and canning.

Materials and Supplies

Wool tweed: ¼ yard, for pouch exterior

Cotton fabric: ¼ yard, for lining

Natural linen or textured solid: scrap, at least ¼ yard, for corners

Fusible fleece: ¼ yard

Various small fabric scraps, for hexagons

1 sheet paper, for hexagons

Zipper: 9″ denim

Thread: clear (invisible) and gray

Zipper pull

Zipper foot and walking foot

Cutting

Templates are on page 117.

Use the pouch template to cut 2 pieces *each* from the wool tweed, lining, and fleece.

Use the corner templates to cut 2 and 2 reverse corner details from the linen.

Use the hexagon template to cut out 5 hexagons from the various fabric scraps, cutting ¼″ outside the edges on all sides.

Use the hexagon template to trace 5 paper hexagon patterns; cut out the paper hexagons along the line.

INSTRUCTIONS

All seam allowances are ¼″.

Make the hexagon appliqué

1. Center and pin a paper pattern on the wrong side of a fabric hexagon. Starting at a corner, fold and hand baste the fabric onto the paper. You'll be hand sewing through the paper. Continue around until all 6 sides of the fabric are folded to the back.

Pin paper to fabric.

Fold one side of fabric over paper; baste.

Continue folding and basting edges.

One completed hexagon

2. Repeat to make 5 hexagons.

3. Place the hexagons right sides together and whipstitch them together in the arrangement shown below. Remove the paper and basting stitches, being careful not to remove any whipstitches.

4. Use a zigzag stitch to machine appliqué the hexagons to the front side of a wool pouch piece. To hide the stitches, use clear thread for the top and gray thread for the bobbin.

Make the pouch

1. Fold and press under the seam allowance along the top edge of the corner details ¼˝. Then, matching up the marks on the template, pin them to the corners of the wool pieces. Topstitch them close to the folded-under edge.

2. Fuse the fleece to the wrong side of both lining pieces, following the manufacturer's instructions.

3. Attach the zipper to the top edge of the wool exterior and lining piece, sewing the pouch together as described on page 17.

4. Attach the zipper fob to the zipper pull.

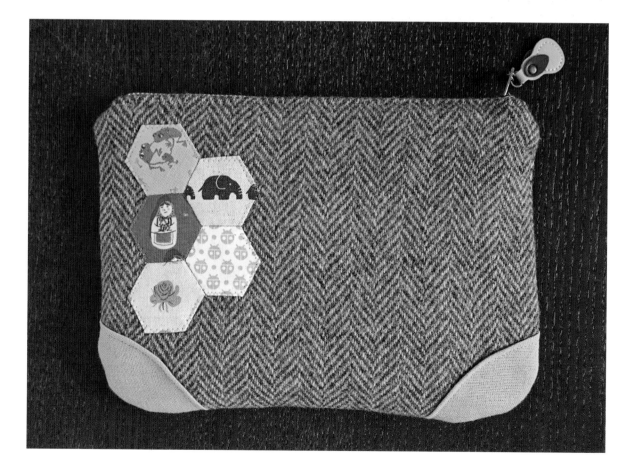

Happy Couple Hand Warmers

Just looking at the happy little faces on these embroidered hand and pocket warmers will warm you up! Adjust the pattern size for the large or little hands in your life.

FINISHED: 4˝ diameter

ARTIST: Holly Keller

WEBSITE:

chezbeeperbebe.blogspot.com

Outfitted with sketchy knowledge of toy design at best and a hand-me-down sewing machine, Holly began designing plushies back in 2005 and named her little company Beeper Bébé. Today, she designs all manner of toys and other things—usually incorporating secondhand or recycled stuff—and she loves to share tutorials on her blog. She has one gorgeously energetic six-year-old boy, who is a continual inspiration (and disruption) to her design endeavors. Holly lives in Minneapolis. Her future goals include moving to France with her family, becoming a cowgirl, finishing that novel she started writing fifteen years ago, learning to quilt, and redesigning Little People for Fisher-Price so they can be as cool again as they once were—not necessarily in that order.

Materials and Supplies

Makes 2 hand warmers.

Unbleached cotton muslin:
½ yard, for embroidery
and hand warmer bags

Red fabric prints: 2 squares
7″ × 7″ each from 2 different
fabrics, for back exterior

**Red, brown, and black
embroidery floss**

Pattern transfer paper

6″ embroidery hoop

1 cup long-grain white rice*

*Do not use short-grain
or quick-cooking rice.*

Cutting

Templates are on page 120.

Unbleached muslin:
Cut 2 squares 8″ × 8″,
for embroidery.

Cut 4 hand warmer full
circles using template.

Red fabric prints:
Cut 4 hand warmer partial
circles using template.

INSTRUCTIONS

All seam allowances are ¼″, unless otherwise noted.

Embroidery

1. Using the pattern transfer paper, trace the embroidery face designs (pages 118 and 119) and outer circles onto the 2 muslin 8″ × 8″ squares (trace the boy face on one and the girl face on the other), centering the design on each.

2. Center a traced muslin square in the embroidery hoop. Use a split stitch and 2 strands of black embroidery thread to embroider the eyes and nose. Use the red thread to embroider the mouth, the cheek circles, and the girl's barrette. Use brown for the hair. Repeat for the other traced design.

3. Cut out the embroidered faces along the outer marked circle.

Assembly

1. Fold under, about ⅛″, the straight edge of each partial circle piece. Fold under again and press. Topstitch the folded edges to secure.

2. Place an embroidered face right side up. Place 2 exterior back pieces on top of the face, right sides together, so the straight edges overlap about ½″ and all the round edges are aligned. Pin. Sew completely around the outer edge, using a ¼″ seam. Clip the curves, being careful not to cut the seams, and turn right side out through the overlapped back. Repeat with the other embroidered face.

3. Align 2 unembroidered muslin circles together and sew around the outer edge, using a ½″ seam and leaving a 2″ opening. Clip the curves, being careful not to cut the seams, and then turn right side out. Fill the pouch with ½ cup rice, then stitch the opening closed. Repeat with the remaining 2 unembroidered muslin circles.

4. Insert the rice-filled bags into the embroidered hand warmer covers through the overlapped back.

USING YOUR HAPPY COUPLE HAND WARMERS

Heat the bags in the microwave for 1–2 minutes to warm them and then insert them in coat pockets to keep hands warm in damp or cold weather.

Patchwork
Pot Holder

Spruce up your kitchen with these round patchwork and linen pot hold-
ers. Clever little pockets in the back protect your hands. Instead of keeping
them in the kitchen, though, why not use them as trivets for a nice hot pot of
afternoon tea? If you use insulated fleece inside, they will protect your table
as well as your hands.

FINISHED: 8½˝ diameter

ARTIST: Kim Kruzich

WEBSITE:

retro-mama.blogspot.com

The daughter of a schoolteacher, Kim grew up with a joy of teaching, and today she shares her love of sewing by designing patterns written so stitchers of all skill levels can make beautiful projects. She is inspired by polka dots, bright colors, and clean, classic lines. Her online shop, Retro Mama, is brimming with fun-to-make patterns, sewing kits, and handmade toys and accessories.

Materials and Supplies

Makes 1 pot holder.

Monochromatic cotton prints: scraps, at least 3″ × 11″ each, of 6 different prints, for patchwork

Natural linen or textured solid: ¾ yard, for backing, pockets, and binding

Natural or gray lightweight cotton twill or canvas: 1 fat quarter, for interlining

Low-loft cotton batting: 12″ × 24″ (or 12″ × 12″ Insul-Fleece by C&T Publishing)

Water-soluble fabric marker

Binding clips

Cutting

Templates are on page 121.

Cotton prints:

Cut 1 strip 1½″ × 10½″, for patchwork strip 1.

Cut 1 strip 1¼″ × 10½″, for patchwork strip 2.

Cut 1 strip 1¾″ × 10½″, for patchwork strip 3.

Cut 1 strip 2″ × 10½″, for patchwork strip 5.

Cut 1 strip 2¼″ × 10½″, for patchwork strip 6.

Cut 1 strip 3″ × 10½″, for patchwork strip 7.

Linen:

Cut 1 strip 1¾″ × 10½″, for patchwork strip 4.

Cut 1 square 11½″ × 11½″, for backing.

Cut 4 partial circle pocket pieces, using template.

Cut 2 linen strips 1½″ × 10″, for pocket single-fold binding.

Cut 1 square 12″ × 12″, for pot holder single-fold bias binding.

Cotton twill or canvas:
Cut 1 square 11½″ × 11½″, for interlining.

Batting:
Cut 2 squares low-loft cotton batting 11½″ × 11½″ (or 1 square 11½″ × 11½″ Insul-Fleece), for interlining.

INSTRUCTIONS

All seam allowances are ¼˝.

Patchwork assembly

1. Arrange the 6 cotton strips in the order listed in the cutting instructions, inserting the 1¾˝ × 10½˝ linen strip as the fourth strip.

2. Sew the strips together to make a large (10½˝ × 10½˝) square. Zigzag stitch the seam allowances along each side of the linen strip. Press the seam allowances toward the darker fabric.

Quilting

1. Layer the 11½˝ × 11½˝ fabric squares in the following order, from bottom to top: linen, twill, 2 batting pieces (or 1 Insul-Fleece). Center the patchwork square on top of the layers. Baste.

2. Quilt as desired by machine or by hand.

3. Using the pot holder template, cut 1 circle 8½˝ in diameter from the quilted patchwork.

Pockets

1. Pin 2 linen partial-circle pocket pieces together and bind the straight edge with 1½˝ × 10˝ single-fold binding (page 25); trim excess binding. Repeat for the remaining pocket pieces.

2. Position the pockets on the linen side of the quilted pot holder, aligning the raw edges and keeping the bound edges parallel. Baste very close to the edge.

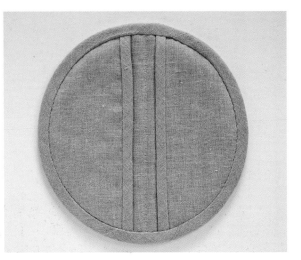

Finishing

1. Make bias binding from the 12″ × 12″ linen square. Cut the square in half on the diagonal (45°) and then cut 2″ strips along the angle. Sew the strips end to end on a diagonal to make at least 30″ of bias tape.

2. Pin the 2″-wide binding around the pot holder edge. Mark the length, with a water-soluble marker, where the end overlaps the beginning by ½″.

3. Cut the end straight on the line, sew the ends together with ¼″ seam to make a continuous circle, and press.

4. Use binding clips to hold the binding onto the pot holder and sew the binding to the pot holder as if binding a quilt (See Single-fold Binding, page 25), using a ⅜″ seam allowance.

Water Bottle Holder

FINISHED: 6˝ tall × 3½˝ diameter

FINISHED STRAP LENGTHS: 13½˝ (short); 52˝ (long)

Linen, appliqué, and embroidery are artfully combined to make a water bottle carrier that's ready to take wherever you go. The interchangeable straps add function as well as high style—hang it, carry it over your shoulder, or shorten the strap to hand carry.

ARTIST: Pascale Mestdagh

WEBSITE:

pm-betweenthelines.blogspot.com

Paris-based Pascale started her blog "Between the Lines" in 2008 as a way to keep in touch with friends and family in faraway places. Soon, however, the blog became a place where she shared her sewing projects and crafts. Now she regularly publishes tutorials on her site. Her designs are simple and elegant. Natural linen, leather, cotton, and wool are her preferred materials.

Materials and Supplies

Natural linen or textured solid: ⅓ yard, for body and straps

Unbleached muslin: ⅓ yard, for body, lining, and long strap backing

Print fabric: ⅛ yard or assorted scraps, for appliqué and short strap backing

Batting: 6″ × 11½″

Buttons: 3 diameter ¾″, for strap attachment

Dark embroidery floss

Water-soluble fabric marker

Sewing machine with button-hole attachment

Cutting

Natural linen:
Cut 1 rectangle 6½″ × 11½″, for body.

Cut 1 strip 1½″ × 41″, for long strap.

Cut 1 strip 1½″ × 14″, for short strap.

Cut 1 circle 3½″ in diameter, for body bottom.

Unbleached muslin:
Cut 2 rectangles 6½″ × 11½″, for body and backing.

Cut 1 strip 1½″ × 41″, for long strap backing.

Cut 1 circle 3½″ in diameter, for lining bottom.

Print fabric:
Cut 1 strip 1½″ × 14″, for short strap backing.

Cut various-sized rectangles, as desired, for appliqué.

INSTRUCTIONS

All seam allowances are ¼".

Body assembly

1. Align the 6½" × 11½" linen rectangle on top of the 6" × 11½" piece of batting, adjusting the linen to overhang the batting equally along the short sides. Pin or baste in place.

2. Fold a 6½" × 11½" muslin rectangle in half lengthwise. Align the folded edge of the muslin along the bottom (11½") raw edge of the batting-lined linen, overlapping the raw edge about ½". Pin the layers together. With embroidery thread, sew the muslin in place along the folded edge, stitching through all the layers, using a running stitch.

3. Use a running stitch to appliqué the print fabric rectangles as desired.

4. Fold the appliquéd body rectangle in half widthwise, right sides facing and aligning the raw edges of the short sides. Sew the short side and press the seam to create a tube. Trim excess batting if necessary.

5. Fold the linen circle in half and again in half. Mark the folds near the raw edge with the water-soluble marker. Pin the linen circle to the bottom raw edges (muslin side) of the body tube, right sides together and using the marks as a reference to distribute the fabric evenly. Sew together. Clip the seam allowance of the curved fabric, being careful not to clip the stitching.

6. Fold the remaining 6½" × 11½" muslin rectangle in half widthwise, aligning the short side edges. Sew the short side seam, starting and stopping to leave an approximately 2" opening halfway along the seam for turning. Press the seam. In the same manner as the body (Step 5), sew the muslin circle to the muslin tube.

7. Slide the muslin lining into the linen body, right sides together, aligning the side seams and raw edges. Pin and sew together at the top edge. Turn right side out through the opening in the lining. Stuff the lining into the body, shape and press.

Strap assembly

1. Align and sew the long 1½″ × 41″ muslin and linen strips together along all sides, right sides together, leaving an opening for turning. Turn, close the opening, shape, and press.

2. Align and sew the shorter 1½″ × 14″ print and linen strips together in the same manner as the long strips (Step 1).

3. Make a ¾″ buttonhole at one end of the long strap and at each end of the short strap.

4. Sew a button to the other end of the long strap.

Finishing

1. Add a running stitch, using embroidery floss, along the top edge of the holder and all the way around both straps.

2. Sew a button to each side of the bottle holder.

3. Add the straps by buttoning the short strap to the body. Lengthen the strap by buttoning one end of the short strap to the long strap, then buttoning the long strap to the body.

An Elephant Never Forgets Bookmark

An elephant never forgets, and these little ladies are certainly unforgettable. Rickrack, buttons, and a crocheted bow give these sweeties all the embellishments they need to help you remember your place. What a great gift for a pal who loves to read!

FINISHED: 6¼″ × 3″

ARTIST: Kat Mew

WEBSITE:

zakkainspired.blogspot.com

Kat plays every day in her teeny tiny craft room in a teeny tiny community in Hawaii. She sews, embroiders, paper crafts, crochets, and twiddles her thumbs. Her aspiration is to find her voice as a zakka crafter, creating her own nonsense, and to seek others like her. If she could have one wish come true, it would be to live in Japan, even for a month or two. This year, she started to focus seriously on zakka-style crafting, inspired by many talented Japanese crafters. And what a journey!

Materials and Supplies

Makes 1 bookmark.

Cotton or cotton/linen blend print: scrap, at least 8½″ × 12″, for head/body and ear

Fusible interfacing: 1 rectangle 8″ × 4½″ (I used Pellon 911FF.)

Button: 1 diameter ⅛″–½″, for eye

Rickrack: 6″ piece, for neck and dress decoration

Water-soluble fabric marker

Optional: Embroidery floss and size 5 (1.9mm) steel crochet hook*, for crocheted bow

Other great choices for the bow are ribbons, lace, or ready-made embellishments.

*Steel crochet hooks have very small hooks for crocheting with thread. Aluminum, plastic, and wood hooks are meant for crocheting yarn and are much too large for this project.

Cutting

Templates are on page 122.

Cotton print:
Cut 2 rectangles 8″ × 4½″, for body.

Cut 2 squares 2½″ × 2½″, for ear.

INSTRUCTIONS

All seam allowances are ¼″, unless otherwise noted.

Ear assembly

1. Trace the ear template on the wrong side of a 2½″ × 2½″ print square piece with a water-soluble marker.

2. Place the 2½″ × 2½″ print squares right sides together. Sew on the traced line with small stitches by hand or machine, leaving a small gap for turning.

3. Trim the seam allowance to ⅛″ and carefully clip the curves. Turn right side out. Press.

4. Sew the opening closed using a ladder stitch (page 98) or your favorite stitch.

Bookmark assembly

1. Fuse interfacing to an 8″ × 4½″ body rectangle, following the manufacturer's instructions.

2. Use a lightbox or window to trace the body template onto the fused interfacing.

3. Add rickrack or lace to the right side of the interfaced body rectangle. Refer to the photo (page 75) for placement options and the traced outline on the back to check positioning. Pin and sew in place.

4. Align the 8″ × 4½″ body rectangles right sides together.

5. Sew along the traced line with small stitches by hand or machine, leaving a 1½″ opening in the back for turning.

6. Trim the seam allowance to ⅛″ and clip the curves around the head, neck, nose, and legs, being careful not to snip any stitches. Clip the fabric between the legs. Trim off the corners of the skirt, nose, and legs. Turn right side out. Press.

7. Sew the opening closed and press again if needed.

Embellishment

The embellishments are attached to only the right side of the elephant. The right side is the side with the interfaced fabric and the nose pointing to the right. This prevents her nose from being squished in the binding of the book! Ouch!

1. Sew a button for an eye to the right side of the elephant.

2. Tack the ear in place with a few blind hem stitches along the top edge.

3. Attach the crocheted bow (below), or other embellishments, with a few hand stitches.

*Optional crocheted bow

Use single crochet (sc) as directed.

Row 1: Using embroidery floss (6 strands), begin the first row with a slipknot, leaving about a 4″ tail. Chain 4, sc in the 2nd chain from hook and in each chain across. Chain 1 and turn. (*3 sc*)

Row 2: Sc in each sc across row.
Chain 1 and turn. (*3 sc*)

Row 3: 2 sc in the 1st sc, sc in remaining sc across row. Chain 1 and turn. (*4 sc*)

Rows 4–9: Sc in each sc across row. Chain 1 and turn. (*4 sc*)

Row 10: Sc, skip 1 sc, sc in remaining sc. Chain 1 and turn. (*3 sc*)

Row 11: Sc in each sc across row. Chain 1 and turn. (*3 sc*)

Row 12: Repeat rows 3 to 9. (*4 sc*)

Row 13: Repeat row 10. (*3 sc*)

Row 14: Repeat row 11. Fasten off, leaving a 7″ tail. (*3 sc*)

With a crochet hook or large-eye needle and the ending tail, connect the 2 ends of the crochet strip by weaving the tail through the top stitches to create a back seam. Flatten the strip with the seam in the middle. Wind the tail 4 or 5 times tightly around the center. Tie the 2 tails at the back of the bow. Weave in the loose ends. Trim any excess.

Patchwork Ribbon

Mix and match the scraps in your stash to create yards and yards of this wonderful patchwork ribbon to keep on hand for oh-so-special and last-minute gifting. Make it your own with simple embellishments like zigzag stitching, buttons, or doilies.

ARTIST: Melody Miller

WEBSITE:

melodymiller.typepad.com

Melody draws, designs, paints, creates, and sparkles at home in Atlanta, Georgia. Her first line of fabric, Ruby Star Rising, was released by Kokka in 2010. She was voted Most Likely to Wear a Prom Dress at the 2010 Houston Quilt Market.

Materials and Supplies

Fabric scraps (a lot of big and small) and/or 2½″ fabric strips (You may use a precut strip bundle, such as a Jelly Roll by Moda.)

Scraps of fabric, trim, lace, and rickrack

Buttons (optional)

Spray starch

INSTRUCTIONS

Wide ribbon

1. If you already have fabric strips (from a precut strip bundle, for example), use these. If not, cut larger pieces of scrap fabric into 2½″ strips (or the width of your choice).

Narrow ribbon

2. Square off any ragged ends and sew the strips together end to end, right sides together, with a ¼˝ seam allowance.

3. Continue adding strips until the ribbon is the desired length. Starch and iron the seams open.

4. Sew small scraps and leftover trim, lace, rickrack, and buttons from other projects to the front of the ribbon. Get creative and use some of the more interesting sewing machine stitches to sew all the way around the scraps. Don't worry about being super neat; let the raw edges show, and have fun!

1. Sort out a pile of fabric scraps that look pretty together.

2. Sew the scraps together, starting with the smallest pieces, until you have a big wonky patchwork block of scraps (mine was approximately 18˝ × 22˝).

3. Starch and iron the block so that it is neat and flat.

4. Use a ruler and rotary cutter to cut the block into 1˝ strips (I cut mine on a diagonal to get the most colors in each strip).

5. Square off the ends of the strips. Sew them together end to end, right sides together, with a ¼˝ seam allowance, until you achieve the desired length. Starch and iron the seams open. At this point, the ribbon is very pretty on the front but messy on the back with all the frayed ends from the patchwork.

6. Fold the ribbon in half widthwise, wrong sides together, matching the 2 short ends.

7. Sew the folded ribbon together along each long side. Use decorative machine stitches, if desired. The frayed edges and patchwork really make this ribbon stand out.

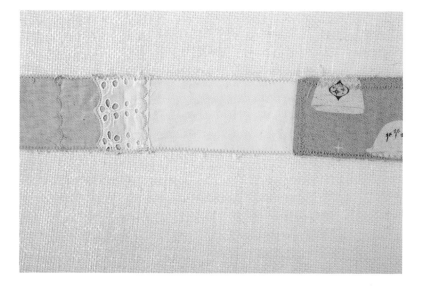

Delightful Linen Bag

FINISHED: 5½″ × 7¼″

How could anyone resist this pouch of pretty patchwork perfection? This cute little sack is wonderful for holding extra essentials. The lovely embellishments can be varied to create your own version of pure delight.

ARTIST: Mette Robl

WEBSITE: erleperle.typepad.com

Mette is a wife and a mom of three who also works part-time as a secretary. Her passion is crafting; she has crafted since she was a teenager and loves it! She's had a blog for six years now and is amazed by how much inspiration one can get through the Internet. She was hooked the first time she discovered the Japanese zakka world—so much inspiration and such fantastic craft supplies from one country!

Materials and Supplies

Natural linen: scrap, at least 8″ × 13″, for bag body

Cotton fabric: scrap, at least 8″ × 13″, for lining

Light-weight sew-in (nonfusible) interfacing: scrap, at least 8″ × 13″″″

1″-wide bias tape: 14″

Fabric scrap: 4″ × 4″

Ribbon: 4″

Crocheted trim: 4″

1 decorative button

Ribbon or synthetic leather: 6″ length, for bag closure

Optional embellishments: Vintage fabrics and trims, lace, cross-stitch, embroidery, buttons, beads, or charms

Cutting

Linen:
Cut 2 rectangles 6″ × 7½″, for body front and back.

Cotton fabric:
Cut 2 rectangles 6″ × 7½″, for lining.

Interfacing:
Cut 2 rectangles 6″ × 7½″, for lining.

INSTRUCTIONS

All seam allowances are ¼˝.

Making the bag

1. Arrange the 4˝ × 4 square fabric scrap, ribbon, crocheted trim, and other fabric embellishments on the front of one 6˝ × 7½˝ linen rectangle. Sew the pieces to the linen using a zigzag stitch. Add additional stitchery, appliqué, or other embellishments, if desired.

2. Align the embellished front and the remaining linen rectangle, right sides together. Sew them together around the sides and bottom edge. Press the seams open. Turn the bag right side out, push out the corners, and press.

3. Place the interfacing on the wrong side of the lining rectangles, then align the lining rectangles, right sides together. Sew around 3 sides and press the seams open.

4. Place the lining into the bag, wrong sides together. Align and pin the top edge.

Finishing

1. Position both ends of the ribbon closure centered on the top back edge, to form a loop. Pin or baste the ends in place so they will not move.

2. Sew the bias tape to the top edge, as if applying double-fold binding to a quilt (page 25). Align the raw edges and start sewing on the back of the bag (to hide the seam), using a ¼˝ seam allowance and being careful to catch the ends of the ribbon closure.

3. Sew the button to the front of the bag.

Now you have your own bag for needles, templates, postcards, or whatever you like.

Bread Basket

FINISHED: 10½˝ wide × 4½˝ high × 3½˝ deep

Sew up this super-cute linen basket for holding warm, yummy mini baguettes, croissants, and more. Make the sides in a solid fabric as shown, or add some patchwork to match your home decor.

ARTIST: Rachel Roxburgh

WEBSITE:

roxycreations.blogspot.com

Australian born and now living in Santarcangelo di Romagna, Italy, Rachel has always loved to make things. Her love has grown ever since she had her daughter and felt the desire to create beautiful things for her. Rachel has always been surrounded by creative people; her mother is a great source of inspiration. Rachel's first passion is textiles, and she usually begins a project because a particular fabric inspires her.

Materials and Supplies

Linen or textured solid: 1 fat quarter, for basket body

Red-and-white check fabric: ½ yard, for handles and lining base

Toile or floral print fabric: 1 fat quarter, for lining

Coordinating fabrics: scraps, at least 2½″ × 2½″, from 3 different fabrics, for patchwork

Accent fabric: scrap, at least 6″ × 4½″, for patchwork

Medium-weight fusible interfacing: ⅓ yard

1 button

Twine or string: ½ yard, for closure loop

Coordinating embroidery floss

Water-soluble fabric marker

Cutting

Linen:

Cut 1 rectangle 2½″ × 5″, for patchwork panel.

Cut 1 square 5″ × 5″, for patchwork panel.

Cut 1 rectangle 11″ × 5″, for back panel.

Red-and-white check fabric:

Cut 4 rectangles 18″ × 4″, for handles.

Cut 2 rectangles 11″ × 4″, for base.

Toile or floral print fabric:

Cut 2 rectangles 11″ × 5″, for lining sides.

Coordinating fabrics:

Cut 1 square 2″ × 2″ from each of 3 fabrics, for patchwork.

Accent fabric:

Cut 2 strips 1¾″ × 5″, for patchwork.

Interfacing:

Cut 1 rectangle 11″ × 4″, for base.

Cut 2 rectangles 11″ × 5″, for front and back panels.

Twine or string:

Cut 3 lengths 5″ each.

INSTRUCTIONS

All seam allowances are ¼˝.

Cutting the handles

1. Refer to the diagram to shape all 4 of the 18˝ × 4˝ handle rectangles. Mark the center of each handle and then measure and mark each side 5½˝ from the bottom edge. Draw a line with a water-soluble marker from each 5½˝ mark to the center of the top edge, slightly rounding the tapered point.

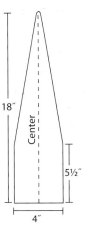

2. Cut the handles to shape along the marked taper line.

Front patchwork panel

1. Arrange and sew the 3 assorted fabric 2˝ × 2˝ squares, right sides together.

2. Sew a 1¾˝ × 5˝ accent fabric rectangle to each side of the patchwork strip.

3. Sew the 2½˝ × 5˝ linen rectangle to one side of the patchwork unit and the 5˝ × 5˝ linen square to the other side, right sides together.

Basket assembly

1. Fuse an 11˝ × 5˝ interfacing rectangle, following the manufacturer's directions, to the wrong side of the patchwork panel and the 11˝ × 5˝ linen rectangle. In the same manner, fuse the 11˝ × 4˝ interfacing rectangle to an 11˝ × 4˝ check rectangle.

2. Use embroidery floss to add running stitches to each side of the patchwork.

3. Sew the linen panels, right sides together, to each long side of the 11˝ × 4˝ interfaced base, making sure to start and stop sewing ¼˝ from each end.

4. Align and sew the squared end of a handle, right sides together, to a raw edge of the just-sewn base. Then align and sew the side panels up the side of the handle to form the box corner for the outer shell. Repeat on the other side of the base. Carefully trim the corners and any excess fabric.

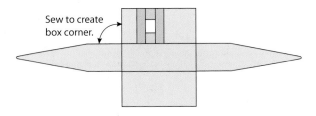

Sew to create box corner.

5. Repeat Step 3 with the 11˝ × 5˝ lining rectangles and the remaining 11˝ × 4˝ base, leaving a 4˝ opening for turning by starting and stopping in the center of one side.

6. Repeat Step 4 to attach the remaining handle pieces to the lining.

7. Braid the 3 pieces of twine. Align the 2 ends of the braid to form a loop. Center the ends along a long edge of the back linen panel. The loop should be facing down in the middle of the back panel (not the patchwork side). Pin or baste in place.

8. Insert the lining into the outer shell, right sides together. Carefully align all the edges and pin in place.

9. Sew around all the raw edges of the basket in a continuous action using a ¼″ seam allowance. *Hint: When sewing the handles, slowly reduce the seam allowance to about ⅛″ when approaching the tapered ends. After stitching the tapered point, slowly increase the seam allowance back to ¼″ when returning to the body of the basket. Do this so you don't lose too much length in the ties.*

10. Trim excess fabric, particularly in the corners where the front and back panels meet the ties. Clip notches around the top of the ties, being careful not to clip the stitches.

11. Turn right side out through the lining opening.

Finishing

1. Push out all the seams and corners; press. Pin in place and topstitch all the way around.

2. Sew the lining opening closed.

3. Sew the button in place at the top center of the front patchwork panel.

4. Knot the handle ties, and the bread basket is complete!

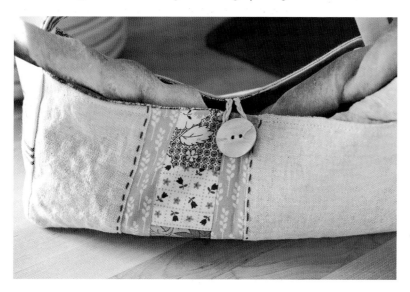

Sweet Sugar Cookie Sack

Every little one loves imaginative play, and who wouldn't with toys like this adorable hand-embroidered sugar cookie set to help them along? Hand-beaded felt cookies in a pretty sack will help your little baker's culinary dreams come true!

FINISHED SACK: 4½˝ wide × 8½˝ tall × 2˝ deep

FINISHED COOKIE: 3˝ diameter

ARTIST: Amy Sinibaldi

WEBSITE:

nanacompany.typepad.com

Amy lives in Los Angeles, California, with her three crazy kids and lovely husband. She is a self-taught crafter who began sewing for the first time in 2006 and is now thoroughly addicted both to creating and to collecting fabric.

Materials and Supplies

Cookie bag:
Makes 1.

Natural linen: scrap, at least 8″ × 21″, for sack body

Cotton print fabric: scrap, at least 5½″ × 5½″, for front patch

Coordinating cotton print fabric: scrap, at least 5″ × 8″, for binding

Ribbon, trim, or twine, for sack tie

Embroidery floss

Playtime cookies:
Makes 6.

1 ecru felt sheet, 9″ × 12″, for cookies

Felt scraps, at least 3″ × 6″ of pink, white, and brown, for cookie frosting

Assorted seed and bugle beads, for cookie sprinkles

Embroidery floss

Polyester fiberfill

Cutting

Templates are on page 123.

Linen:
Cut 2 rectangles 7″ × 10″, for sack body.

Cotton print:
Cut 1 rectangle 5″ × 5″, for front patch.

Coordinating print:
Cut 2 strips 7″ × 2″, for binding.

Ecru felt:
Cut 12 circles using the cookie template.

Felt scraps:
Cut 2 frosting shapes using the template, from *each* of 3 colors, for cookie frosting.

INSTRUCTIONS

All seam allowances are ¼˝.

Embroidered patch

1. Use the template to trace the frame and "Sugar Cookie Mix" onto the center of the front patch. Embroider the patch using running and stem stitches in coordinating colors.

2. Center the design and trim the embroidered patch to 4˝ × 3½˝. Center the patch on a linen rectangle with the bottom (7˝) edge approximately 2½˝ from the bottom edge of the linen. Pin in place.

3. Hand stitch the patch to the linen, using a blind stitch and tucking under a ¼˝ hem. Or use a machine stitch, pressing under the ¼˝ hem on all 4 sides before pinning in place and stitching as close to the edge as possible.

Bag assembly

1. Use the 7˝ × 2˝ strips to bind the top (7˝) edge of each linen rectangle, as if applying a single-fold binding (page 25) to a quilt, using a ½˝ seam allowance.

2. Align the linen rectangles, right sides together, with the bound edges at the top. Pin and sew along both sides and the bottom.

3. Pinch the bottom corners together, lining up the side and bottom seams. Use a ruler and pencil to draw a line measuring 1˝ from the point and perpendicular to the seam allowance. Pin and stitch along the line. Trim off the corner to ½˝. Repeat with the other corner.

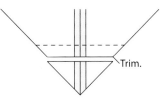

Trim.

4. Serge or zigzag stitch all the seams to finish them.

5. Turn the sack right side out. Push out the corners and press.

6. Fill the sack with polyester fiberfill, or cut-up rags, if desired. Tie with ribbon, string, or twine.

Cookie assembly

1. Center 1 piece of frosting felt onto 1 circle of cookie felt. Sew individual beads to the frosting through both layers of felt, using a double strand of matching floss and securing the knots to the back side of the cookie felt. Start attaching the "sprinkle" beads in the center of the frosting and work toward the edges for a natural look. Repeat to make 6 cookie tops.

2. Place a completed cookie top, right side up, onto an unfrosted cookie circle. Sew around the edges of the layered cookie, using matching embroidery floss and a blanket stitch, and leaving about a 1˝ opening. Stuff with polyester fiberfill so the cookie is squishy but not puffy; then finish sewing the edges. Knot and bury the thread ends.

Little Pocket Pillowcase

Your little one will surely sleep soundly with this sweet little pillow beneath his or her precious head. Tucked into a colorful diamond patchwork pocket is a cute little friend to keep your wee one company. Change the dimensions to suit your pillows for a perfect fit.

FINISHED: 17½″ × 11″

ARTIST: Meg Spaeth

WEBSITE: elsiemarley.com

Meg is a mother of three little children and considers herself very lucky to have a wonderful husband. When she was younger, she worked as a baker and then as a chocolatier. After having children she left the professional kitchen but continued to cook and bake for her family. Meg wanted to make things that would have more permanence than a soufflé, so she learned to sew again and found herself making clothes, toys, and quilts—and having a wonderful time. The amazing and supportive craft community she found through her blog has helped her learn to make so many things and inspired her to make more.

Materials and Supplies

White linen or cotton: ⅞ yard, for pillowcase

Assorted cotton scraps: a variety totaling ¼ yard, for diamond patchwork and bear's belly

¼˝ piping cord: ¾ yard

Wool felt (or felted wool sweater): 1 fat quarter, for bear body

Embroidery floss

Wool or polyester stuffing

Toddler pillow: 16˝ × 12˝

Cutting

Templates are on page 124.

White linen:
Cut 1 piece 12˝ × 25˝, for main part of pillowcase.

Cut 2 pieces 6˝ × 12˝, for pillowcase hem.

Cut 1 piece 11½˝ × 12˝, for pillowcase hem.

Cut 1 piece 6˝ × 6˝, for pocket lining.

Scraps:
Cut 54 diamonds from template.

Wool:
Cut 2 bear bodies from template.

Cut 4 bear arms from template.

INSTRUCTIONS

All seam allowances are ¼˝, unless otherwise noted.

Pocket patchwork

1. Arrange 30 diamonds using the layout diagram at right.

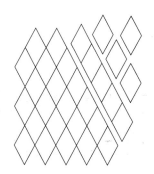

2. Sew the diamonds together in diagonal rows, using a ¼˝ seam allowance, as shown. Press the seams in one direction.

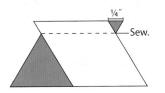

3. Sew the rows together, trying to match the points of the diamonds as accurately as possible. Press the seams in the same direction.

4. Trim the diamond patchwork to measure 6˝ × 6˝ square.

5. Align the diamond patchwork with the 6˝ × 6˝ pocket lining square, right sides together, and sew the top edge only.

6. Flip the lining to the back of the patchwork, so the wrong sides are together, and press the seam.

Pillowcase hem

1. Place the patchwork pocket, right side up, on top of a 6˝ × 12˝ linen strip (right side up), aligning the bottom (6˝) raw edges.

2. Align the other 6˝ × 12˝ linen strip on top of the first strip, right sides together, with the pocket in between. Pin.

3. Sew along the right side edge (the right edge of the pocket) using a ¼˝ seam. Fold the top lining to the back and press to set the seam.

4. Open the piece flat with the pocket on the left side, as shown below. Place the 11½˝ × 12˝ piece of linen on top, right sides facing.

5. Sew a ½˝ seam along the top and bottom edges to create a tube.

6. Trim the seam allowance to ¼˝, turn right side out, and press.

Main pillowcase

1. Fold the 12˝ × 25˝ piece of linen in half widthwise, as shown below, wrong sides together.

2. Sew the 2 sides together with a French seam: With the pillowcase right side out, sew a ¼˝ seam and trim the seam allowance to ⅛˝. Turn the pillowcase inside out, press, and sew ¼˝ again from the edge. Turn the pillowcase right side out again and press. This should completely enclose the seams with a finished edge.

Patchwork piping

1. Sew 20 diamonds together in a long row. It should be at least 25˝ long; if not, add more diamonds.

2. Press the seams in one direction.

3. Fold in half lengthwise; press.

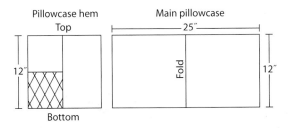

4. Tuck the piping cord into the fold and sew a basting stitch down the length of the patchwork strip as close to the cord as possible (using a zipper foot helps).

5. Trim the seam allowance to ¼″.

Pillowcase assembly

1. Pin the piping on the right side of the main pillowcase opening, raw edges lined up.

2. Attach the ends of the piping by folding under the raw edge of one end and inserting the other end into the fold. Remove some of the previous stitches and piping cord, to help join the ends smoothly; then trim the excess.

3. Baste the piping to the main pillowcase.

4. Slide the pocket side of the hem tube around the open end of the pillowcase, right sides together. Align the raw edges of the pocket and lining fabrics and match the hem seams with the main pillowcase. Pin in place.

5. Sew the hem to the pillowcase, staying as close to the

piping cord as possible (a zipper foot is helpful).

6. Open the hem right side out and press the seam toward the hem.

7. Press under the raw edge on the hem ¼″.

8. Fold the hem in half toward the inside of the pillowcase and press.

9. Turn the pillowcase inside out and hand stitch the hem to the pillowcase, just beyond the piping seam.

10. Insert a pillow into the pillowcase.

Bear

1. Sew 2 sets of 2 diamonds together, as before (see Pocket Patchwork, Steps 2 and 3, page 93). Sew the sets together to make a large diamond. Cut into an oval shape using the template.

2. Appliqué the oval onto the belly on the right side of a bear body. Embroider eyes and a nose on the same body piece.

3. Align 2 arm pieces together, right sides facing. Sew around the curve, leaving the straight edge open, and turn right side out. Repeat for the other arm.

4. Lightly stuff the arms and pin them in place on the appliquéd body, aligning the raw edges and positioning them facing in toward the belly.

5. Align the appliquéd body onto the other body piece, right sides together. Sew all around the bear, leaving a 2″ opening for stuffing.

6. Clip the curves, turn right side out, and stuff with wool or polyester stuffing. Hand stitch the opening closed.

Sweet Memories
Photo Frame

Make photo memories even more special with this adorable handmade picture frame, lovingly made with stamping, patchwork, and rickrack detailing. You could easily make these in several sizes to fill your home with memories and handmade goodness.

FINISHED: 5¾" × 7⅜"

ARTIST: Ayumi Takahashi

WEBSITE:
ayumills.blogspot.com

Throughout her childhood in Japan and adulthood in America, Ayumi always loved making everything from scratch. She's been into sewing, soap-making, herbal remedies, miniature-making, and cooking. Sewing is her definite favorite—especially zakka-inspired items! She lives in northern California with her sweetest hubby, Joe.

Materials and Supplies

Print fabrics: 20 assorted scraps, at least 3″ × 2″, for patchwork

Natural linen or textured solid: ¼ yard, for base and frame

Backing fabric: scrap, at least 8″ × 10″

Lightweight polyester batting: ⅛ yard

Chipboard (0.022″ or 0.024″ thickness): 8½″ × 11″, for frame base

Sashiko thread or embroidery floss: 3 yards

Craft paper: 1 sheet 8½″ × 11″, for photo tabs

1 cereal box (standard size), for cardboard backing

1 decorative button, for embellishment

³⁄₁₆″-wide leather string: 4″, for hanger

¼″-wide rickrack: ½ yard

Fabric glue

Spray adhesive, such as Elmer's Craftbond

Optional: ¼″ alphabet stamps and textile ink pad, for stamping

Cutting

20 assorted print fabric scraps:
Cut 1 piece 2″ × 1¼″ from each fabric, for patchwork.

Natural linen:
Cut 4 pieces 2″ × 1¼″, for patchwork.

Cut 2 strips 1½″ × 4½″, for frame top and bottom.

Cut 1 piece 7¼″ × 9″, for frame base.

Backing fabric:
Cut 1 piece 7¼″ × 9″, for frame back.

Lightweight polyester batting:
Cut 2 pieces 1″ × 7¼″, for frame sides.

Cut 2 pieces 1″ × 3½″, for frame top and bottom.

Chipboard:
Cut 2 pieces 1″ × 7¼″, for frame sides.

Cut 2 pieces 1″ × 3½″, for frame top and bottom.

Cut 1 piece 5¾″ × 7⅜″, for frame base.

Continued on next page

Craft paper:

Cut 1 piece 1½″ × 4″, for bottom photo tab.

Cut 2 pieces 1½″ × 6″, for side photo tabs.

Cereal box cardboard:

Cut 1 piece 5¾″ × 7⅜″, for frame backing.

Rickrack:

Cut 2 strips 7½″ long.

INSTRUCTIONS

All seam allowances are ¼″.

Frame border assembly

1. Sew the 2″ × 1¼″ printed fabrics together, along the long (2″) edges, to create 2 patchwork strips, each consisting of 10 fabrics and measuring 2″ × 8″.

2. Sew a 2″ × 1¼″ linen piece to each short end of the patchwork strips.

3. Place a 1″ × 7¼″ piece of batting on top of a piece of chipboard the same size. Center a patchwork strip on the batting. Then, using sashiko thread, hand sew the folded-back edges to the back of the padded chipboard as shown. Repeat for the other patchwork strip.

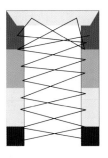

4. Repeat Step 3, using the 1½″ × 4½″ linen pieces and the 1″ × 3½″ chipboard and batting pieces, to create the frame top and bottom.

5. Use a ladder stitch to sew together the top/bottom and patchwork sides to make the frame border. A curved needle will be helpful for this process.

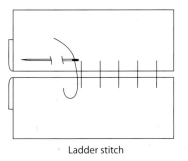

Ladder stitch

6. Fold the 1½″ × 4″ piece of craft paper in half lengthwise. Apply glue to an outer side of the paper. Attach it to the wrong side of the frame, centered along the bottom edge about ½″ away from the frame opening, and with the folded edge facing the outer edge of the frame. Repeat to attach the 1½″ × 6″ paper strips to each side.

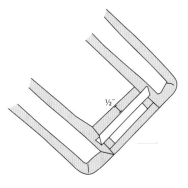

Frame base assembly

1. Apply spray adhesive, following the manu-facturer's directions, onto the wrong side of the 7¼″ × 9″ piece of linen. Center the 5¾″ × 7⅜″ piece of chipboard on the wrong side of the linen and fold the edges of the linen to the back of the chipboard. Set it aside.

2. Apply spray adhesive onto the wrong side of the 7¼″ × 9″ piece of backing fabric. Center the 5¾″ × 7⅜″ cereal box cardboard on the wrong side of the backing and fold the fabric edges to the back of the cardboard.

3. Glue rickrack to the long sides of the covered cardboard.

4. Hand sew the leather string to the right side of the covered cardboard, close to the top edge.

5. Complete the frame base by applying spray adhesive to the wrong side of the covered cardboard and attach, wrong sides together, to the covered chipboard (from Step 1).

6. Apply glue to the wrong side of the patchwork frame border, along the outer edges of the 2 sides and bottom. Apply a small amount of glue to the craft paper tabs. Attach this to the linen side of the frame base and let dry.

Embellishment

1. Stamp the frame border as desired and hand sew a button on top of the frame.

2. Insert a photo at the top of the frame between the patchwork border and the base, positioning the photo in the paper tabs to center it.

Pleated Coin Purse

FINISHED: about 4½˝ × 5˝

This design brings a crafty classic into modern times. The charming coin purse with a purchased metal frame features sweetly appealing pleating.

ARTIST: Karyn Valino

WEBSITE: theworkroom.ca

Karyn has always loved to make things. She did bookbinding, photography, woodworking, stained glass, and neon sign-making before falling in love with sewing. She created the workroom, a sewing lounge/ shop in Toronto, Canada, to share this love with a larger community. Karyn's personal blog, makesomething.ca, is where she shares her personal craft and sewing projects.

Materials and Supplies

Midweight cotton: 1 fat quarter, for purse exterior

Cotton print: 1 fat quarter, for lining

Batting: 2 scraps, at least 6˝ × 7˝ each

Curved metal purse frame: 2¾˝ wide × 2˝ tall*

Glue that will bond to both fabric and metal (such as Weldbond)

Awl or similar tool

Nylon pliers

Water-soluble or chalk marker

Purse frames available online at theworkroom.ca.

Cutting

Templates are on page 125.

Midweight cotton:
Cut 2 pieces from exterior template; mark notches and fold lines.

Cotton print:
Cut 2 pieces from lining/batting template; mark notches.

Batting:
Cut 2 pieces from lining/ batting template.

INSTRUCTIONS

All seam allowances are ¼".

Purse exterior

1. Fold an exterior piece along the left fold line, right side facing up. Match the fold to the left match line. Pin the pleat in place at the top and bottom. Do the same with the right fold and match lines. Repeat with the other exterior piece.

2. Press the pleats flat. Stitch the pleats down, starting at the top of the fold line and sewing 1″ down, very close to the folded edge. Then sew up 1″ from the bottom of the fold line, very close to the folded edge. Repeat for each pleat.

3. Align and pin the exterior pieces, right sides together. Start at the right side notch and sew downward from the right side notch, along the bottom edge to the left side notch, leaving the top curve open. Clip the curves on the sewn seam allowance. Turn the purse right side out. Smooth out the seam allowance from the inside and press flat.

Lining

1. Baste a batting piece to the wrong side of a lining piece with a ⅛″ seam allowance. Repeat for the other side.

2. Align and pin the lining pieces, right sides together. Start at the right side notch and sew downward from the right side notch, along the curve, stopping at the right bottom notch. Continue sewing from the left bottom notch and stop at the left side notch, leaving the top curve open and an opening in the lining for turning.

Assembly

1. Slip the purse exterior (right side facing out) into the lining (wrong side facing out), so the right sides are together. Line up all the raw edges along the top curves on each side and pin in place. Sew one side of the purse at a time; starting from a side notch, sew around the top curve to the other side notch. Repeat on the other side.

2. Clip the curves. Then turn the purse right side out through the lining opening and carefully press out the curves.

3. Sew the lining opening closed by hand or machine.

4. Press flat each side of the purse top curve.

Purse frame

1. Put glue along the inside of one side of the metal purse frame. Carefully slide one side of the purse top curved opening into the metal frame. Use an awl to push the fabric into the frame on all sides. Wipe away any excess glue. Let this dry for 5–10 minutes before repeating with the other side.

2. Using a pair of nylon pliers (or cover metal pliers with tape or foam so you don't scratch the frame), pinch the frame near the hinge, on both sides, to secure the frame in place.

3. Allow the glue to dry completely, at least 24 hours, before using the coin purse.

Happy Garland
Message Board

What could be better than an adorable message board made using an embroidery hoop? A message board with tiny colorful bunting and clothespins, of course! This project can be made with a large or small hoop. Put these organizers around your home to hold all your messages and reminders.

FINISHED: 10˝ diameter

ARTIST: Katrien Van Deuren

WEBSITE:

abitofpillipilli.blogspot.com

Katrien is the girl behind the
world of pilli pilli. She has a
degree in philosophy, is a little
addicted to traveling, and
firmly believes in enjoying the
simple things in life, such as
the sunshine in her bedroom
on a summer Sunday morning,
or a pretty cup from which to
drink her coffee. Making things
has been an important part of
her life for as long as she can
remember. As a child, her bedroom was her atelier. Katrien
would sit on the floor and cut
and paste a whole new world
around herself. She never antici-
pated, of course, that now, 25
years later, she would still be
doing the exact same thing, and
call it "work"!

Materials and Supplies

Assorted fabric scraps: at least 2″ × 2″, for garland appliqués

Natural heavyweight linen or textured solid: 1 square 15″ × 15″,
for base

Fusible fleece: 1 square 15″ × 15″

Acrylic felt: 1 square 11″ × 11″, for back

10″ wooden embroidery hoop

Fabric glue

Thick string or twine: 20″

Medium-sized wooden spring clothespins

Cutting

Assorted fabric scraps:
Cut 17 triangles ¾″ × 1″ × 1″.

Acrylic felt:
Cut a 9¾″-diameter circle (or trace the inner circle of your
embroidery hoop to determine the exact size and shape).

INSTRUCTIONS

Appliqué

1. Iron the fusible fleece, following the manufacturer's directions, to the back of the linen fabric.

2. Arrange the triangles to create 2 "string" rows of garlands on the linen. Pin in place.

3. Sew the triangles onto the linen by machine, using black thread. First, sew a straight line across the whole length of the garland row, starting and stopping at least 2" past the end of the string of garlands to make the end of the string "disappear" under the wooden hoop after framing. Then stitch around the triangles following the V-shaped outline.

4. *Optional:* Add a small bow at the end of one (or both) of the garlands, using a free-motion machine embroidery technique. Alternatively, embroider the bow by hand.

Board assembly

1. Arrange thick string across the linen base to form a "clothesline" underneath the garlands.

2. Center the piece in the wooden embroidery hoop and smooth the surface by pulling gently at the excess fabric. Tighten the hoop with the screw.

3. Trim the excess fabric and fusible fleece into a circle around the hoop, leaving a 2" allowance for gluing.

4. Carefully peel the fusible fleece from the 2" allowance of fabric. Cut away this excess fusible fleece to reduce the bulk.

5. Fold the 2" allowance over the hoop toward the back and glue in place.

Finishing

1. Glue the felt circle to the back of the hoop.

2. Use thick string to tie a little bow at the end of the clothesline.

3. Add the wooden clothespins.

Leave a message!

Nesting Boxes

FINISHED: 4″, 5″, and 6″ boxes

"A place for everything and everything in its place"—that's what comes to mind with this trio of nesting boxes. Measuring 4″, 5″, and 6″, and embellished with patchwork, embroidery, and appliqué delights, these will spruce up your place in high zakka style.

ARTIST: Laurraine Yuyama

WEBSITE: patchworkpottery.com

Laurraine is a self-taught quilter who creates her own designs and patterns. She has fun combining elements from her two passions—patchwork and pottery—to create dishes with patches of intricate patterns, and quilted three-dimensional objects like teapots and tea-cups. Many of her sophisticated country designs incorporate machine appliqué, hand embroidery, and buttons. She is greatly inspired by tea, Japanese country patchwork, and the online craft community where she is known as PatchworkPottery. Laurraine's patterns have been published internationally in seven books to date, and she creates patterns for magazines in Canada and Taiwan. She sews, blogs, and sells her pattern booklets online from her bright attic studio in New Westminster, British Columbia, Canada.

Materials and Supplies

Makes 3 boxes.

Natural linen or textured solid: ⅞ yard for backing, bottom, and lining

Coordinating print fabrics: a variety to total ½ yard for sides and leaf appliqués

High-loft batting: 26″ × 28″

Embroidery floss: match print fabrics

White chalk marking pencil

Walking foot and darning/embroidery foot

Cutting

	LARGE BOX (6″)	MEDIUM BOX (5″)	SMALL BOX (4″)
LINEN	4 @ 4½″ × 6½″, for sides; 1 @ 8″ × 26″, for backing; 2 @ 6½″ × 6½″, for bottom	4 @ 3″ × 5½″, for sides; 1 @ 7″ × 22″, for backing; 2 @ 5½″ × 5½″, for bottom	4 @ 4½″ × 4½″, for bottom and sides; 1 @ 6″ × 18″, for backing
PRINT FABRICS	12 @ 2½″ × 2½″, for sides; 2 *each* of 4 different fabrics @ 3″ × 4″, for large leaf appliqués; Bias strip 2″ × 25″, for binding	8 @ 3″ × 3″, for sides; 2 *each* of 4 different fabrics @ 2½″ × 3½″, for small leaf appliqués; Bias strip 2″ × 21″, for binding	8 @ 2½″ × 2½″, for sides; 2 *each* of 2 different fabrics @ 2½″ × 3½″, for small leaf appliqués; Bias strip 2″ × 17″, for binding
BATTING	1 @ 8″ × 26″, for side; 1 @ 8″ × 8″, for bottom	1 @ 7″ × 22″, for side; 1 @ 7″ × 7″, for bottom	1 @ 6″ × 18″, for side; 1 @ 6″ × 6″, for bottom

INSTRUCTIONS

All seam allowances are ¼˝. Small, medium, and large boxes each have different patchwork designs.

Block and side panel assembly

Large Box (6˝)

This box has the same design on all 4 sides.

1. Sew together 3 print squares 2½˝ × 2½˝. Press the seams to one side.

2. Sew the pieced strip to a 4½˝ × 6½˝ linen rectangle along the 6½˝ edges. Press the seams toward the linen.

3. Repeat Steps 1 and 2 to make 4 blocks.

4. Join the 4 blocks to make a strip 6½˝ × 24½˝. Press the seams open.

Medium Box (5˝)

This box has the same design on all 4 sides.

1. Sew together 2 print squares 3˝ × 3˝. Press the seam to one side.

2. Sew the pieced strip to a 3˝ × 5½˝ linen rectangle along the 5½˝ edges. Press the seam toward the linen.

3. Repeat Steps 1 and 2 to make 4 blocks.

4. Join the 4 blocks to make a strip 5½˝ × 20½˝. Press the seams open.

Small Box (4˝)

This box has patchwork on 2 sides and appliqué only on 2 sides.

1. Sew together 4 print squares 2½˝ × 2½˝ to create a Four Patch. Repeat to make 2 blocks.

2. Join the 2 blocks alternately with 2 linen squares 4½˝ × 4½˝, as shown in the photo, to make a strip 4½˝ × 16½˝. Press the seams open.

Leaf appliqués

Templates are on page 126.

1. Trace a large leaf shape from the template on the back of a print 3˝ × 4˝ rectangle. With right sides together, match with a rectangle of the same fabric.

2. Sew on the line around the entire shape. Trim with pinking shears or cut notches around the curves.

3. Carefully cut a slit in one side and turn right side out. Press.

4. Repeat Steps 1–3 to make 4 large leaves from the 3˝ × 4˝ rectangles (for large box) and 6 small leaves from the 2½˝ × 3½˝ rectangles (for medium and small boxes).

Quilting and appliqué

Use the quilting designs from the templates on pages 126 and 127, or use your own designs.

1. For each box, arrange the layers as follows: Place the linen rectangle, right side up, on top of the batting. Then, center the side panel, right side down, on top of the linen rectangle. Pin the layers in place.

2. Sew along the side and bottom edges of the pieced side panel, leaving the top edge open.

3. Trim excess batting and backing at the sides and bottom, and trim the sewn corners at an angle. Do not trim the top edge. Turn right side out. Press.

4. Pin baste using safety pins at the centers of the blocks. Using a walking foot and starting from the bottom (sewn) edge, stitch in-the-ditch of every seam.

5. Mark a dot using white chalk in the center of each print fabric patch. Use this as a reference point to center the flower quilting design.

6. Use a darning or embroidery foot to quilt a flower shape in each print fabric patch, returning to the dot after each petal. (This can also be done with a regular foot.) Use the larger design for the large box and the smaller design for the medium and small boxes.

7. Position and pin each leaf onto a linen patch. (The larger leaves are for the large box.) Topstitch the leaf to the linen using a leaf vein design. Starting at the base of the leaf, sew down the center of the leaf to the tip. Turn and sew the side veins on the way back. Sew back and forth over the lines several times to create depth.

Embroidery and binding

1. Using 6 strands of embroidery floss and a running stitch, sew down the sides of the linen patches. Refer to the various project photos for the positioning of the lines on each box.

2. Align binding strips to the top (unfinished) edge of the side panels. Fold under the short ends of the binding a ¼″ and pin in place. Sew in place as if attaching a single-fold binding to a quilt (page 25). Trim the batting, leaving an extra ¼″ of batting and backing. Fold the binding over to the back and whipstitch in place.

Bottom assembly

1. Align and pin 2 linen bottom squares of the same size, right sides together. Place the layered squares onto their corresponding batting square.

2. Sew around the edge of the linen squares, leaving a 3″ opening on one side. Trim excess batting and trim the corners.

3. Turn right side out and sew the opening closed.

4. Topstitch ⅜″ in from the edge.

5. Mark and quilt a large flower design on the bottom, as in Quilting and Appliqué, Steps 5 and 6 (page 112).

Box assembly

1. Hand sew the ends of the side panel together using a whipstitch.

2. Hand sew the side panel to the corresponding bottom.

3. Press the edges of the box.

Finished!

Templates

THE HOUSE POUCH

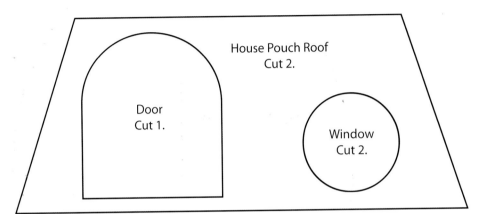

House Pouch Roof
Cut 2.

Door
Cut 1.

Window
Cut 2.

Enlarge 200%.

RAIN CLOUD MUG RUG

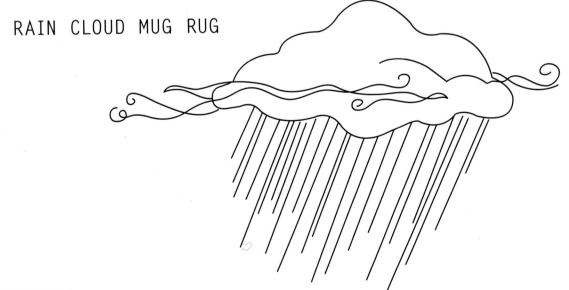

STEM MESSENGER BAG

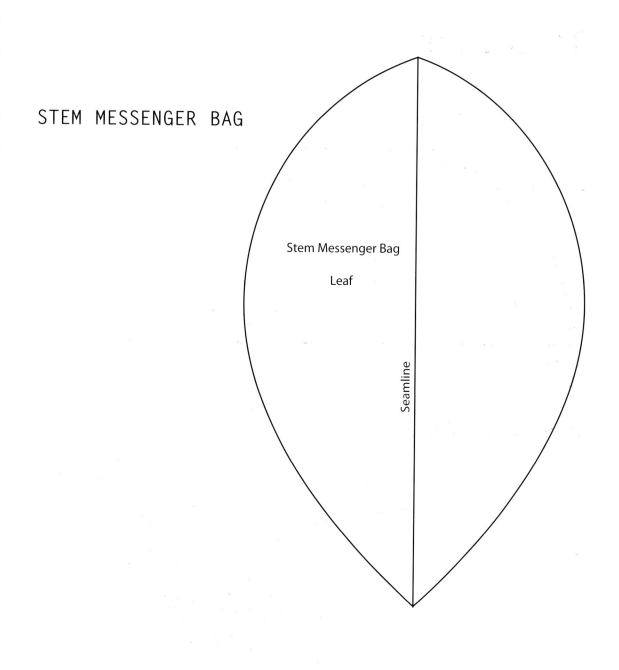

Stem Messenger Bag

Leaf

Seamline

STEM MESSENGER BAG, CONT'D

Stem Messenger Bag
Flap Curved Corner

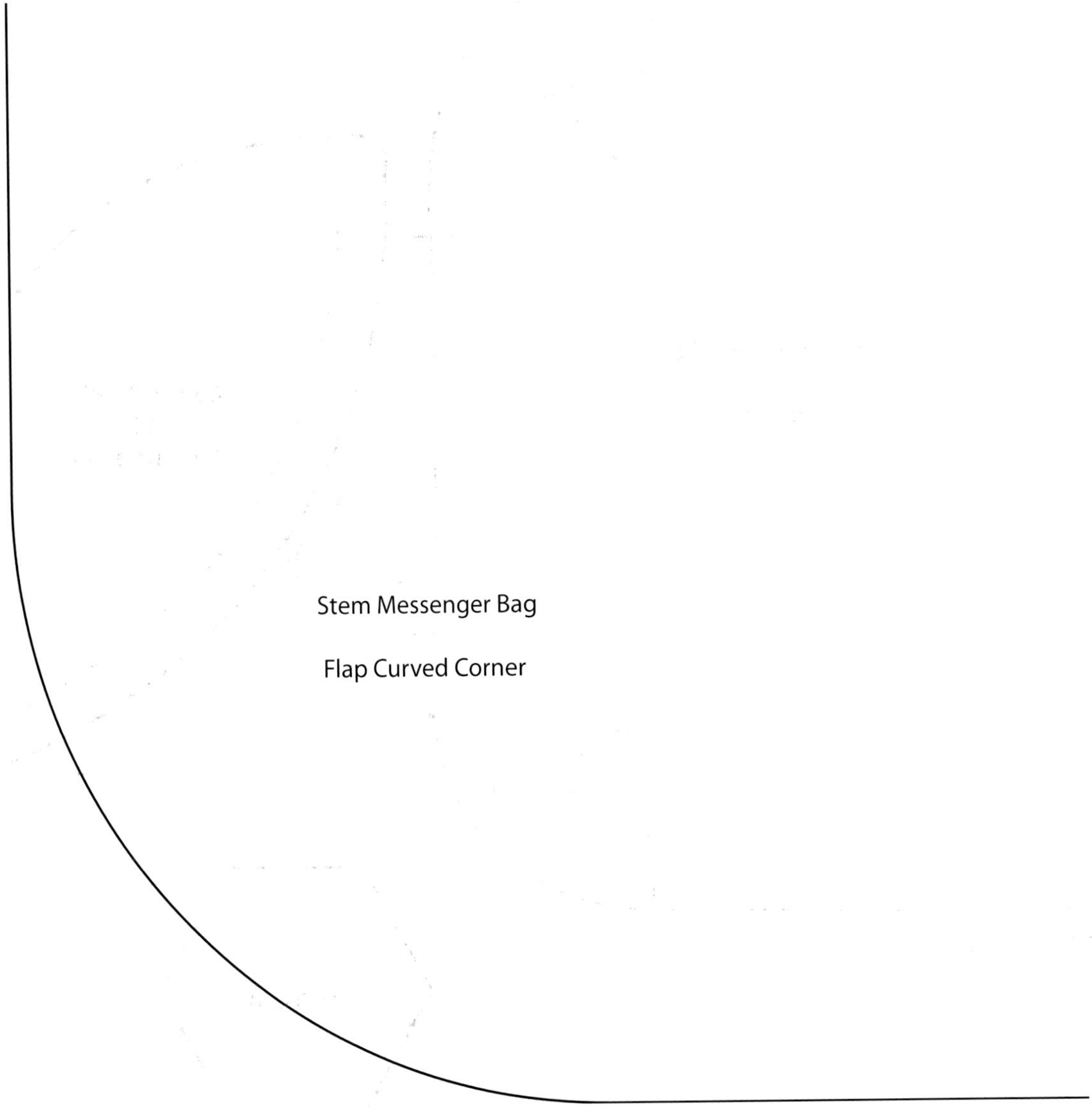

ORCHARD PATH TWEED POUCH

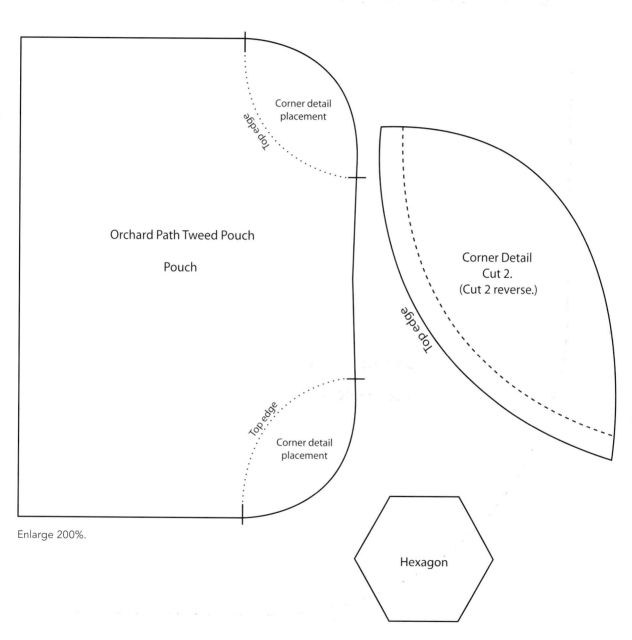

Corner detail
placement

Top edge

Orchard Path Tweed Pouch

Pouch

Top edge

Corner detail
placement

Corner Detail
Cut 2.
(Cut 2 reverse.)

Top edge

Enlarge 200%.

Hexagon

HAPPY COUPLE HAND WARMERS

Embroidery Face Design (girl)

Embroidery Face Design (boy)

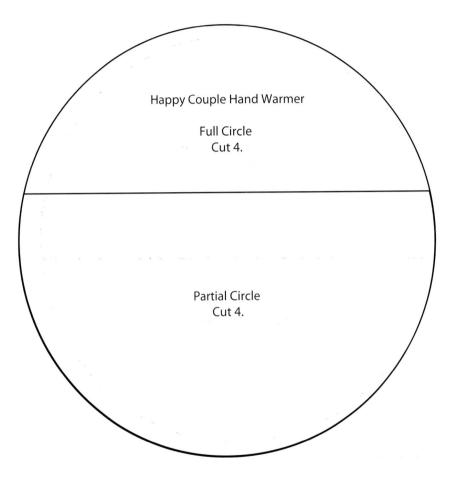

Happy Couple Hand Warmer

Full Circle
Cut 4.

Partial Circle
Cut 4.

PATCHWORK POT HOLDER

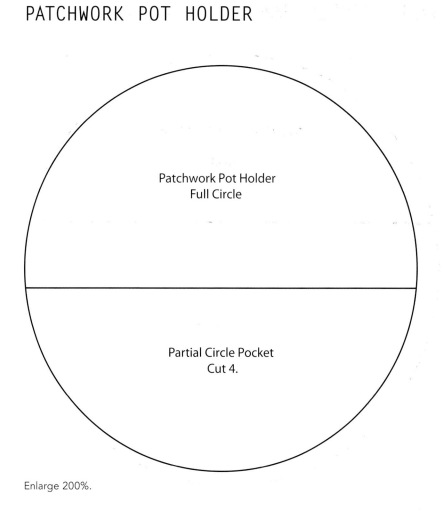

Patchwork Pot Holder
Full Circle

Partial Circle Pocket
Cut 4.

Enlarge 200%.

AN ELEPHANT NEVER
FORGETS BOOKMARK

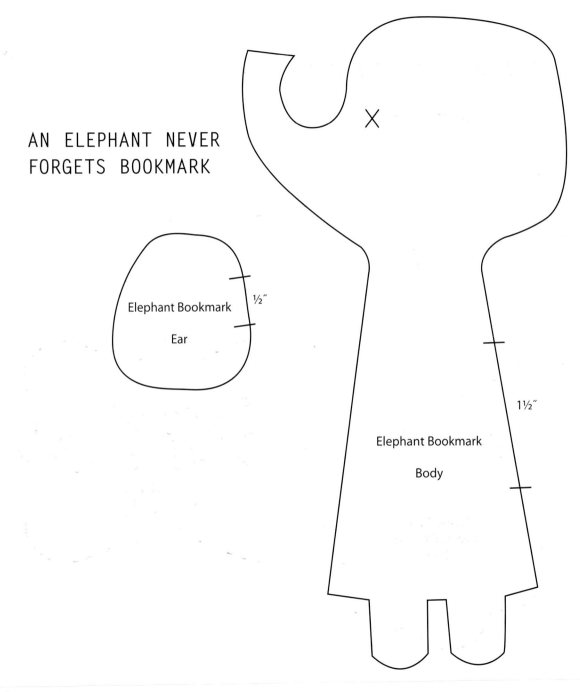

Elephant Bookmark

Ear

½″

Elephant Bookmark

Body

1½″

SWEET SUGAR COOKIE SACK

Sweet Sugar Cookie
Cut 12.

Sweet Sugar
Cookie Frosting
Cut 6.

SUGAR
cookie
MiX

LITTLE POCKET PILLOWCASE

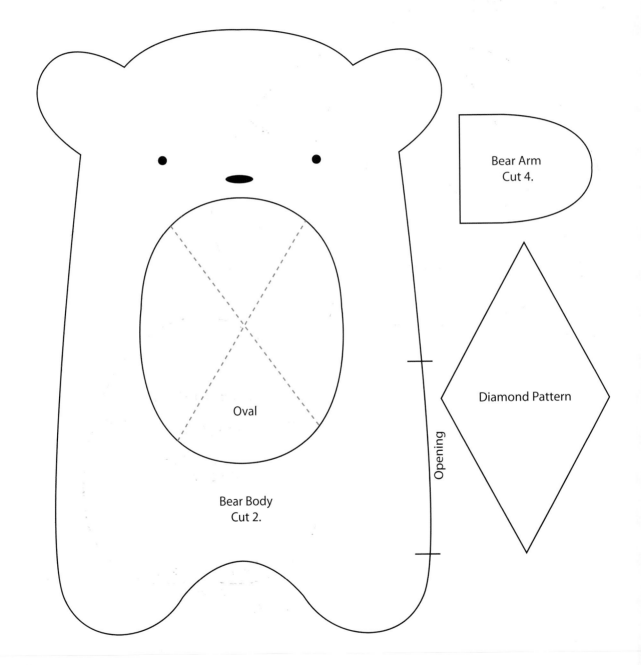

Bear Arm
Cut 4.

Diamond Pattern

Opening

Oval

Bear Body
Cut 2.

PLEATED COIN PURSE

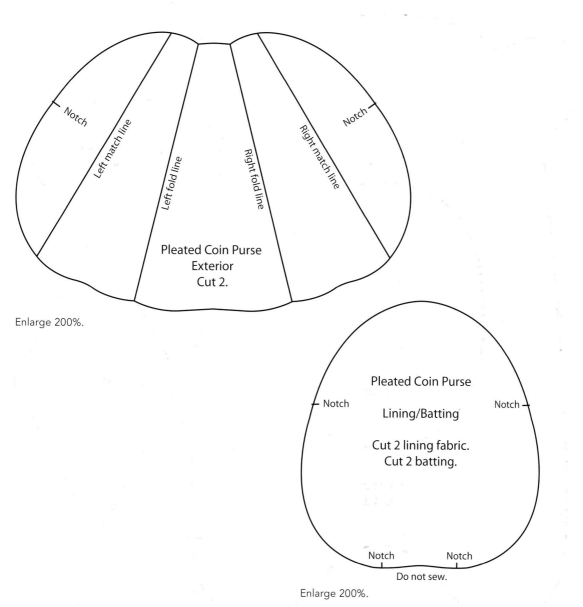

Notch

Left match line

Left fold line

Right fold line

Right match line

Notch

Pleated Coin Purse
Exterior
Cut 2.

Enlarge 200%.

Notch

Pleated Coin Purse

Lining/Batting

Cut 2 lining fabric.
Cut 2 batting.

Notch

Notch

Notch

Do not sew.

Enlarge 200%.

NESTING BOXES

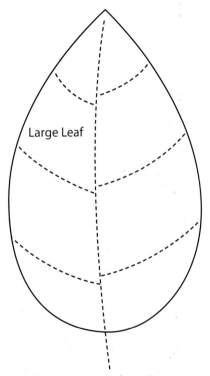

Large Leaf

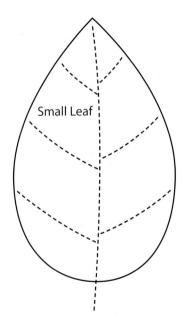

Small Leaf

- - - - Dashed lines are for quilting.

Bottom Flower Quilting Design

Small Side Flower Quilting Design

Large Side Flower Quilting Design